# Gender, Migration and the Media

This volume brings together a number of experts who explore conceptual and policy challenges, as well as empirical realities, associated with gender and migration in highly mediated societies. The need to more systematically address the gendered experience of migration, especially in relation to political and cultural representation, is in the core of the discussions that unfold in this book. The book's chapters address a number of critical questions in relation to the representation of women as members of communities and as outsiders in culturally diverse societies. In doing so, the collection pays particular attention to the sphere of media and communications. Mediated communication has become crucially important in the construction of meanings of identity and citizenship, while the media have taken centre stage in framing debates on migration, border control and gender representations in culturally diverse societies. *Gender, Migration and the Media* presents a cross-cultural and interdisciplinary understanding of the practices and the consequences of mediated communication for identity and citizenship.

This book was originally published as a special issue of *Ethnic and Racial Studies*.

**Myria Georgiou** teaches in the Department of Media and Communications at the London School of Economics (LSE), UK. Her research focuses on questions of identity construction within mediated urban and transnational spaces. Previous publications include *Transnational Lives and the Media: Reimagining Diasporas* (2007) and *Diaspora, Identity and the Media: Diasporic Transnationalism and Mediated Spatialities* (2006).

**Ethnic and Racial Studies**
Series editors: Martin Bulmer, *University of Surrey, UK,* and John Solomos, *City University London, UK*

The journal *Ethnic and Racial Studies* was founded in 1978 by John Stone to provide an international forum for high quality research on race, ethnicity, nationalism and ethnic conflict. At the time the study of race and ethnicity was still a relatively marginal sub-field of sociology, anthropology and political science. In the intervening period the journal has provided a space for the discussion of core theoretical issues, key developments and trends, and for the dissemination of the latest empirical research.

It is now the leading journal in its field and has helped to shape the development of scholarly research agendas. *Ethnic and Racial Studies* attracts submissions from scholars in a diverse range of countries, fields of scholarship and crosses disciplinary boundaries. It has moved from being a quarterly to being published monthly and it is now available in both printed and electronic form.

The Ethnic and Racial Studies book series contains a wide range of the journal's special issues. These special issues are an important contribution to the work of the journal, where leading social science academics bring together articles on specific themes and issues that are linked to the broad intellectual concerns of *Ethnic and Racial Studies*. The series editors work closely with the guest editors of the special issues to ensure that they meet the highest quality standards possible. Through publishing these special issues as a series of books, we hope to allow a wider audience of both scholars and students from across the social science disciplines to engage with the work of *Ethnic and Racial Studies*.

Other titles in the series include:

**The Transnational Political Participation of Immigrants**
*Edited by Jean-Michel Lafleur and Marco Martiniello*

**Anthropology of Migration and Multiculturalism**
*Edited by Steven Vertovec*

**Migrant Politics and Mobilisation: Exclusion, Engagements, Incorporation**
*Edited by Davide Però and John Solomos*

**New Racial Missions of Policing: International Perspectives on Evolving Law-Enforcement Politics**
Edited by Paul Amar

**Young People, Ethnicity and Social Capital**
Edited by Tracey Reynolds

**Cosmopolitan Sociability**
Edited by Tsypylma Darieva, Nina Glick Schiller and Sandra Gruner-Domic

**Retheorizing Race and Whiteness in the 21st Century**
Edited by Charles A. Gallagher and France Winddance Twine

**Theorising Integration and Assimilation**
Edited by Jens Schneider and Maurice Crul

**Ethnic and Racial Minorities in Asia: Inclusion or Exclusion?**
Edited by Michelle Ann Miller

**Diasporas, Cultures and Identities**
Edited by Martin Bulmer and John Solomos

**Gender, Race and Religion: Intersections and Challenges**
Edited by Martin Bulmer and John Solomos

**Latino Identity in Contemporary America**
Edited by Martin Bulmer and John Solomos

**Migration: Policies, Practices, Activism**
Edited by Martin Bulmer and John Solomos

**Nationalism and National Identities**
Edited by Martin Bulmer and John Solomos

**Methods and Contexts in the Study of Muslim Minorities: Visible and Invisible Muslims**
Edited by Nadia Jeldtoft and Jørgen S. Nielsen

**Irregular Migrants: Policy, Politics, Motives and Everyday Lives**
Edited by Alice Bloch and Milena Chimienti

**Fighting Discrimination in Europe: The Case for a Race-Conscious Approach**
Edited by Mathias Möschel, Costanza Hermanin and Michele Grigolo

**Responses to Stigmatization in Comparative Perspective**
Edited by Michele Lamont and Nissim Mizrachi

**Health Care and Immigration: Understanding the Connections**
Edited by Patricia Fernandez-Kelly and Alejandro Portes

**Gender, Migration and the Media**
Edited by Myria Georgiou

**Accounting for Ethnic and Racial Diversity: The Challenge of Enumeration**
*Edited by Patrick Simon and Victor Piché*

**Methodologies on the Move: The Transnational Turn in Empirical Migration Research**
*Edited by Anna Amelina, Thomas Faist and Devrimsel D. Nergiz*

# Gender, Migration and the Media

*Edited by*
Myria Georgiou

LONDON AND NEW YORK

First published 2013
by Routledge
2 Park Square, Milton Park, Abingdon, Oxfordshire OX14 4RN

Simultaneously published in the USA and Canada
by Routledge
711 Third Avenue, New York, NY 10017
First issued in paperback 2014

*Routledge is an imprint of the Taylor and Francis Group, an informa business*

© 2013 Taylor & Francis

This book is a reproduction of *Ethnic and Racial Studies*, volume 35, issue 5. The Publisher requests to those authors who may be citing this book to state, also, the bibliographical details of the special issue on which the book was based.

All rights reserved. No part of this book may be reprinted or reproduced or utilised in any form or by any electronic, mechanical, or other means, now known or hereafter invented, including photocopying and recording, or in any information storage or retrieval system, without permission in writing from the publishers.

*Trademark notice*: Product or corporate names may be trademarks or registered trademarks, and are used only for identification and explanation without intent to infringe.

*British Library Cataloguing in Publication Data*
A catalogue record for this book is available from the British Library

ISBN 978-0-415-63101-3 (hbk)
ISBN 978-1-138-84490-2 (pbk)

Typeset in Times New Roman
by Taylor & Francis Books

**Publisher's Note**
The publisher would like to make readers aware that the chapters in this book may be referred to as articles as they are identical to the articles published in the special issue. The publisher accepts responsibility for any inconsistencies that may have arisen in the course of preparing this volume for print.

# Contents

*Citation Information* ix
*Notes on Contributors* xi

1. Introduction
   *Myria Georgiou* 1

## Part I: Conceptual and policy interrogations

2. Access denied: the anatomy of silence, immobilization and the gendered migrant
   *Katharine Sarikakis* 10

3. Getting integration right? Media transnationalism and *domopolitics* in Ireland
   *Gavan Titley* 27

4. Do Turkish women in the diaspora build social capital? Evidence from the Low countries
   *Christine Ogan and Leen d'Haenens* 44

5. Intersectionality and mediated cultural production in a globalized post-colonial world
   *Isabelle Rigoni* 61

## Part II: Engendered diasporic mediascapes

6. Watching soap opera in the diaspora: cultural proximity or critical proximity?
   *Myria Georgiou* 77

7. Online mediations in transnational spaces: cosmopolitan (re)formations of belonging and identity in the Turkish diaspora
   *Miyase Christensen* 97

8. Migrant African women: tales of agency and belonging
   *Olga Guedes Bailey* 115

## CONTENTS

9. Identities in-between: the impact of satellite broadcasting on Greek Orthodox minority (Rum Polites) women's perception of their identities in Turkey
*Asli Tunç and Ariana Ferentinou*   133

*Index*   151

# Citation Information

The chapters in this book were originally published in *Ethnic and Racial Studies*, volume 35, issue 5 (May 2012). When citing this material, please use the original page numbering for each article, as follows:

**Chapter 1**
*Introduction*
Myria Georgiou
*Ethnic and Racial Studies*, volume 35, issue 5 (May 2012) pp. 791-799

**Chapter 2**
*Access denied: The anatomy of silence, immobilization and the gendered migrant*
Katharine Sarikakis
*Ethnic and Racial Studies*, volume 35, issue 5 (May 2012) pp. 800-816

**Chapter 3**
*Getting integration right? Media transnationalism and domopolitics in Ireland*
Gavan Titley
*Ethnic and Racial Studies*, volume 35, issue 5 (May 2012) pp. 817-833

**Chapter 4**
*Do Turkish women in the diaspora build social capital? Evidence from the Low countries*
Christine Ogan and Leen d'Haenens
*Ethnic and Racial Studies*, volume 35, issue 5 (May 2012) pp. 924-940

**Chapter 5**
*Intersectionality and mediated cultural production in a globalized post-colonial world*
Isabelle Rigoni
*Ethnic and Racial Studies*, volume 35, issue 5 (May 2012) pp. 834-849

# CITATION INFORMATION

**Chapter 6**
*Watching soap opera in the diaspora: Cultural proximity or critical proximity?*
Myria Georgiou
*Ethnic and Racial Studies*, volume 35, issue 5 (May 2012) pp. 868-887

**Chapter 7**
*Online mediations in transnational spaces: cosmopolitan (re-)formations of belonging and identity in the Turkish diaspora*
Miyase Christensen
*Ethnic and Racial Studies*, volume 35, issue 5 (May 2012) pp. 888-905

**Chapter 8**
*Migrant African women: Tales of agency and belonging*
Olga Guedes Bailey
*Ethnic and Racial Studies*, volume 35, issue 5 (May 2012) pp. 850-867

**Chapter 9**
*Identities in-between: The impact of satellite broadcasting on Greek Orthodox minority (Rum Polites) women's perception of their identities in Turkey*
Asli Tunç and Ariana Ferentinou
*Ethnic and Racial Studies*, volume 35, issue 5 (May 2012) pp. 906-923

# Notes on Contributors

**Miyase Christensen** is Professor of Media and Communication Studies at Karlstad University, Sweden, and researcher for the Department of Philosophy and History of Technology at the Royal Institute of Technology (KTH) in Sweden.

**Leen d'Haenens** is Professor in the Centre for Media Culture & Communication Technology, Catholic University of Leuven, Belgium, and Lecturer in the Department of Communication Studies at Radboud University Nijmegen, the Netherlands.

**Ariana Ferentinou** is Lecturer in the Media and Communication Systems Department at Istanbul Bilgi University, Turkey.

**Myria Georgiou** teaches in the Department of Media and Communications at the London School of Economics (LSE), UK. Her research focuses on questions of identity construction within mediated urban and transnational spaces.

**Olga Guedes Bailey** is Senior Lecturer in the School of Arts and Humanities, Institute of Cultural Analysis at Nottingham Trent University, UK.

**Christine Ogan** is Professor Emerita in the School of Journalism and the School of Informatics at Indiana University, USA.

**Isabelle Rigoni** is a Researcher at MIGRINTER-CNRS in Poitiers, France and MICA-CNRS in Bordeaux, France.

**Katharine Sarikakis** is Professor of Media Governance at the Institute of Communication Studies, the University of Vienna, Austria.

**Gavan Titley** is Lecturer in the School of English, Media and Theatre Studies at the National University of Ireland, Maynooth, Ireland.

**Asli Tunç** is Associate Professor in the Media and Communication Systems Department at Istanbul Bilgi University, Turkey.

# Introduction

Myria Georgiou

**Abstract**
Mediated representations of gender, ethnicity and migration play an increasingly important role in the way these categories are understood in the public sphere and the private realm. As media often intervene in processes of individual and institutional communication, they provide frameworks for the production and consumption of representations of these categories. Thus media – in their production, representations and consumption – need to be analysed, not only as reflections as pre-existing socio-political realities, but also as constitutive elements in the production of meanings of the self and the *Other*. This special issue includes a number of articles that examine the articulations of gendered ethnic identities and of gendered citizenship as these are shaped in media production, media representations and media consumption.

**Introduction**

Debates on media's role in the cultural and political representation of ethnicity and gender are not unknown to scholars of race and ethnicity. This is the case especially in culturally-diverse societies where political struggles for minorities' visibility, rights and recognition have a long history and a current relevance. In fact, media have often been summoned and held to account about their role in influencing public opinion on issues of culture, 'race', gender and citizenry. More than ever, this becomes a familiar public discourse at times of crisis. At other times, media are less often discussed, sidelined in public debates about participation, inclusion and citizenship. Yet it is the permanence and invisibility of the media in everyday life and their taken-for-granted authority that sustains media power. Media are as ordinary as they are ever-present in social, political and cultural life, becoming almost invisible as cultural and political agents. Our growing dependence on knowing about the world and about each other through media representations reaffirms and reproduces media's symbolic power. Thus, media need to be understood not just as reflections of reality but also in their role in constructing reality (Couldry 2000).

As the social world is increasingly colonized by the media (Silverstone 1994), we need to understand how media contribute to framing meanings of the self, the *Other*, the society we live in. We locate this special issue within scholarship that studies media as 'resources for thought, judgment and action, both personal and political' (Silverstone 2007, p. 5). This scholarship gains particular relevance at times of intense public debates on the 'failure of multiculturalism', the intensification of border control, and the feminization of migration. How central is the role of media in framing these debates? Do alternative and community media challenge hegemonic discourses of ethnic and gender stratification? And how much do uses and appropriations of media and communications counter-balance social and political exclusion and marginalization? Addressing these questions requires research in all elements of the media system: media production, representation (content), and media consumption.

The articles in this special issue come out of research on different elements of the media system and their regulation. Some of them have a primary focus on cultural life (identity) and others on political life (citizenship). Yet they all aim to understand the ways in which media and communications become involved in power struggles around the representation and recognition of women migrants and refugees.

The discussions and analyses presented here recognize the distinctiveness of each element of the media system (production, representation, consumption), as well as two kinds of important continuities: between different elements of the media system and between minority media worlds and the broader socio-cultural context where they are located. The first continuity is 'internal'. The institutional basis of the media informs the ways representations are framed, while regulation of the media and of everyday life shape the context and limits of their consumption, argue du Gay et al (1997) in their definition of the *circuit of culture*. Media power does not just trickle down from the producers through media representations to consumers. It is a social process 'reproduced in the details of what social actors do and say' (Couldry 2000, p. 4) and is more complex than a lineal model of media transmission implies. The second 'external' continuity refers to the relation between minority and mainstream media and the voices they represent. While our focus here lies on the ways in which ethnic minority and migrant women are present (or absent) in media production, representations and consumption, we also recognize that this communicative space is not fully distinct and separate from the wider communicative spaces where these groups are located. The diversity of media production, experiences of exclusion and inclusion, and the various patterns of consumption in contemporary societies all represent elements of a single media environment, a media ecology, writes Silverstone (2007). Consequently we can only grasp the meanings of minority media worlds in their contrapuntal relation to other media systems they address or contradict, as much as we can only understand mainstream media when we register their contrapuntal relationship to the experiences, voices and practices of the included and the excluded (but still present) minorities (ibid.). Thus, the debates that unfold in the following pages are not about *Other* and distinct media worlds, but about elements of the complex media world we all occupy in culturally-diverse societies.

## An interdisciplinary crossroad: gender, migration and the media

As Downing and Husband (2005) argue, there are many good reasons why we should be worried about media's role in shaping meanings of race and ethnicity in culturally-diverse societies. In liberal democracies, media often claim their role as the fourth estate of the realm (ibid.). Research and public debates have repeatedly emphasized the importance of the free flow of information in democratic deliberation and the representation of diverse interests in the society (Dahlgren 2009). In supporting the exchange of ideas and information thus, media support civil society and provide systems of control of the state. At least this is the case according to the idealized liberal democratic model of media function. How much is this ideal a reality?

The position that different groups take in the mediation processes – as producers, as consumers, as neither or both – has multiple implications for participation in communication and, to a significant extent, to the wider social and political processes. The struggles around the control of media, technologies, and systems of representations have become more intense with the emergence of different players in the terrain of mediated communication, especially with the wide diffusion of new technologies. Though the web, Twitter, mobile phones and other personal media challenge existing hierarchies, we are far from celebrating the full democratization of mediated communication. Television, and national media more generally, retain their central and influential role in popular culture and in framing public debates around migration, ethnicity and gender. Something has changed though and this is not just the technological terrain. While 'old' media have great cultural and political influence, their authority is now, more than ever perhaps, conditional.

New forms of mediated communication are now as ordinary and banal as once television was. Recording the diversity of outlets is not in itself enough to understanding what the shift from mass-communication to mass self-communication (Castells 2009) actually means. The diversity of outlets gives voice to ideologies, which are not necessarily (though sometimes they are, indeed) contained within the ideological systems of the nation-state and the dominant media corporations. New technologies allow communication from many to many outside the system of dominant and established media (ibid.). While media power remains unequally concentrated in the hands of the few, the level of autonomy among alternative, minority and community media has noticeably increased.

There is no doubt that the diffusion of communication technologies has benefited migrant, diasporic and other dispersed groups. There is also no doubt that the fragmentation of media spaces (with personal media and social media, for example) also diversified communication within migrant and diasporic groups. Women, often marginalized, alongside other internal minorities within ethnic communities, are given some new opportunities for voicing their interests and alternative sets of representations against hegemonic ones widely circulating within ethnic communities and the broader society. This diversification, Cunnigham argues (2001), advances the emergence of public sphericules. A dystopia and an indication of the end of the public sphere for Gitlin (1998), public sphericules reflect the changing public sphere, not a destruction of it (Cunningham 2001). For minorities and for minorities within minorities, cultural connections, transnational networks and affiliations with multiple spheres and sphericules present elements of a complex system of communication that can advance participation and recognition (ibid.) unlike the exclusive and excluding national public sphere where the demonstration of singular loyalties is often a requirement.

It is in this networked and fragmented space of mediated transnational communication that possibilities for multiple identities and expanded meanings of citizenship can be observed. When it comes to migrant and refugee women this is a particularly important area of study, since often these are groups that face multiple forms of marginalization from the public sphere: as a result of their ethnicity, lack of citizenship rights, and gender relations within their own ethnic group and the broader society.

*Media power and resistance*

In an ERS special issue on Feminism and Postcolonialism, Suki Ali argued:

> the need to think through issues of 'race', ethnicity and class as situated within globalized networks of economic, cultural and technological expansion is central to feminist discussions of power and resistance, as it is of course to feminist politics and practice (2007, p. 197).

In similar ways as Ali emphasizes the need to locate globalized networks at the core of feminist analysis of power, media and communications research on networked mediated communication needs to relocate 'race', ethnicity and gender in its analyses of (media) power. A set of shared key empirical and conceptual questions underlie the study of 'race', ethnicity and gender, especially questions of recognition, (mis)representation, stereotyping and visibility. It is in this context that two framing points for the analysis of gender, migration and the media need to be highlighted.

Intersectionality provides a necessary analytical framing concept for understanding how gender, ethnicity and 'race' become intertwined in the construction of meanings of identity and citizenship through the media. There is significant evidence in our research that demonstrates how these categories and the mediated construction of their meanings intersect. The second point is that of another kind of intersectionality, that between the different elements of the media system. Media production, content and consumption represent not only elements of the media system but also interrelated elements of a social field where meanings of ethnicity, 'race' and gender take their shape.

The dominance of white, middle-class men in the management and production of the media is well recorded in feminist media and communications literature (Gill 2009; Ross 2009). The intersectionality of specific gender, class and 'racial' identities in newsrooms has reproduced the concentration of symbolic power in the hands of social elites with consequences not only for female and male professionals of minority backgrounds but also for the outputs of these media. With decision power in the media remaining stubbornly concentrated in the hands of elites, hegemonic racial and gender ideologies have become repeatedly reproduced and circulated in the society and habitually accepted as 'truth'. Tuchman (1978) influentially argued that women are symbolically annihilated in the media through omission, condemnation and trivialization. Arguably this applies to other minority groups, like ethnic minorities and refugees. As Tuchman adds, if a group is absent or trivialized in the media then it becomes easier to believe that it doesn't exist, it doesn't matter or only matters when it fits appropriate roles (e.g. beautiful, in the case of women or 'integrated' in the case of ethnic minorities).

The reoccurrence of particular representations of women and ethnic minorities in the media also reproduces stereotypes. Media stereotypes confirm social and political hierarchies Lippmann wrote in the early days of mass media ((1922) 2007), and his thesis still remains relevant. Representing difference in the media in a fair, realistic and coherent manner has never been an easy task and it has raised concerns among academics and activists since the 1970s (cf. Hartman and Husband 1974; Hall 1977). Critical cultural studies has for long discussed media's role in misrepresenting social injustice and attributing problems such as crime to the behaviour of specific (ethnic) groups (Hall 1977).

As all media represent specific ideological interests it would be naïve to try to locate resistance by looking at the production and content of the media alone. The point of media consumption and appropriation reflects the point of meaning-making and interpretation of the diffused media messages. Audiences are also citizens or hopeful citizens. In an interconnected world, media can provide new tools to minorities for seeking visibility and a voice. New media give opportunities to some marginalized groups to seek new roles as producers of their own messages. Yet, the vast majority of people are on the receiving side of representations of gender, 'race' and ethnicity. Everyday life is the space where the hegemonic ideologies of gender, ethnicity and 'race' becomes diffused, accepted but also resisted.

**Locating a transnational debate**

We here explore cases where media create spaces for deliberation and provide opportunities for groups and individuals to locate themselves, to become visible and heard. We also examine cases where media reproduce minorities' social marginalization and ethnic and gender stratification. But we also explore some of the ways in which media outside the mainstream resist but also sometimes reproduce hegemonic systems of racial and gender stratification.

The regulation of migrants' and refugees' access to systems of communication is in the core of the two first papers in this volume by Sarikakis and by Titley. Individuals' and groups' sense of belonging in a society can be supported or restricted by both media and state mechanisms, argues Titley. With a focus on Ireland, Titley argues that this country's short-lived integration regime deployed culture and interculturalism as resources for the self-governing integration of all foreign nationals, while at the same time developing a system of civic stratification designed to limit claims to citizenship and social and economic rights. Titley argues that migrants largely depend on transnational media in managing tensions associated with social exclusion and possibilities of participation.

Sarikakis focuses on asylum seeker detention centres and examines the effect that loss of communication rights under detention immobilizes and silences migrants, especially women. Sarikakis investigates the process of silencing and immobilization of migrants and the particular forms it takes for female migrants through disenablement of communicative acts. The state of exceptionality assigned to detained migrants is supported in the criminalization of migration laws and securitization, which together with widespread policies of incarceration in the west have become the antipode of the fundamental principles of free movement and expression, she concludes.

Locating these debates in the city, the articles by Chistensen and by Bailey examine the gendered experiences of migration in city spaces. While their studies have very different starting points, with Christensen focusing on online communication and Bailey on interpersonal community communication, they both demonstrate the *placeness* of identities. With reference to Turkish migrants in Stockholm and their use of online social networks, Christensen examines expressions of identity and belonging as these are shaped at the intersection of online communicative practice and offline locality. With a focus on the specificities of gendered constructions of sociality and subjectivity in the diaspora, Christensen reclaims the significance of place in the study of mediated and transnational communication. Media, she argues, do not necessarily detach identities from place, but rather relocate them in it.

With a focus on African asylum seeker and refugee women in the British city of Nottingham, Bailey's study demonstrates some of the ways in which these women develop systems of everyday gendered resistance to the destitution, lack of cultural recognition, and gender inequality. Her study examines these systems of resistance through an ethnography of a women's NGO which provides them with a collective and safe 'home' space. Bailey argues that the NGO, established by the women for themselves, represents significant evidence on how local grassroots movements challenge the invisibility of asylum-seekers' and refugees' lives and reflect an expanded notion of politics with community and solidarity in its core.

Rigoni turns to ethnic community media as institutions that provide space of solidarity and community but which also become involved in struggles around gender and class power. For this reason, Rigoni emphasizes the significance of intersectionality as an important conceptual tool to analyse practices of cultural production in ethnic minority media. Drawing from empirical research on female journalists' experience in ethnic media, she reveals the contradictory realities of work in ethnic media. On the one hand, she demonstrates how ethnic media often reproduce gender and class hierarchies observed in other kinds of media. On the other, she refers to cases where women have found spaces of expression and emancipation in such media, especially when these are constructed primarily as female initiatives (e.g. minority women's magazines). The paper juxtaposes media research with gender studies and ethnic studies in order to understand these internal contradictions of gender roles within minority media.

Ogan and D'Haenens locate the struggles around female sociality and recognition within the social world that migrant women occupy in the Netherlands and Flanders, Belgium. Their study of migrant women's social capital comes at a time when cross-European debates on the 'failure of multiculturalism' intensify. Critics of multiculturalism have located the problems associated with cultural diversity on the retreat of ethnic minorities within their own separate ethnic worlds. Ogan and D'Haenens examine the accuracy of these claims. They particularly examine the relevance of arguments according to which minorities, especially women, would be better integrated if they build social capital by bridging to people and institutions in their new countries and by adopting the 'shared values' of the host countries.

For the Greek Orthodox Christian women in Istanbul who Tunç and Ferentinou study, satellite television plays a key role in building social capital. In a series of interviews with female members of this group, Tunç and Ferentinou observe that satellite television provides core material for sustaining a sense of identity between the very local, grounded and urban experience of Istanbul and a transnational cultural community of Greek Orthodox people. For this group of heavy viewers of the Greek satellite television channels, television provides the primary link to Greece but also a daily companion that helps them manage isolation and regional nationalistic ideologies.

With a focus on a different group of female television viewers, Georgiou examines how soap opera consumption supports Arab women's efforts to manage conflicting cultural ideologies. Georgiou studies Arab women in London and their consumption of the female-oriented genre of soap opera on Arabic language satellite television. The paper shows that soap opera viewing provides female audiences in the diaspora with opportunities to reflect on their own identities as distant from hegemonic discourses of gender in their region of origin but as proximate to a moral set of values they associate with this same region. As this is especially, but not exclusively, the case with young women born in the diaspora, it becomes apparent that gender identities in culturally-diverse societies are in flux.

The discussions that unfold in this special issue demonstrate some of the ways in which personal and group experiences and understandings of identity and citizenship are located in historical and political contexts. Media do not just observe and report on the context of political and policy debates. Media often provide frames for understanding what these categories mean. They channel authority to speak and rights to be heard. And sometimes they also leave space for voices to be heard when they otherwise get no access to the public sphere. As such, a focus on the media is not peripheral but core to understanding the challenges associated with governance and cultural life in societies of difference.

## References

ALI, SUKI 2007 'Introduction: Feminism and Postcolonial: Knowledge/Politics, *Ethnic and Racial Studies*, vol. 30, pp. 191–212
CASTELLS, MANUEL 2009 *Communication Power*, Oxford: Oxford University Press
COULDRY, NICK 2000 *The Place of Media Power: Pilgrims and Witnesses of the Media Age*, London: Routledge
CUNNINGHAM, STUART 2001 'Popular media as public "sphericules" for diasporic communities', *International Journal of Cultural Studies*, vol. 4, pp. 131–47
DAHLGREN, PETER 2009 *Media and Political Engagement*, Cambridge: Cambridge University Press
DOWNING, J.OHN and HUSBAND, C.HARLES 2005 *Representing 'Race': Racisms, Ethnicities and Media*, London, Thousand Oaks, New Delhi: Sage
DU GAY, PAUL (ed.) 1997 *Doing Cultural Studies: The Story of the Sony Walkman*, London: Sage
GILL, ROSALIND 2009 *Gender and the Media*, Cambridge: Polity
GITLIN, TODD 1998 'Public sphere or public sphericules?', in T. Liebes and J. Curran (eds), *Media, Ritual and Identity*, London: Routledge, pp. 175–202
HALL, STUART 1977 'Culture, the media and the ideological effects', in J. Curran, M. Gurevitch and J. Woollacott (eds), *Mass Communication and Society*, London: Arnold
HARTMANN, PAUL and HUSBAND, CHARLES 1974 *Racism and the Mass Media*, London: Davis-Poynter
LIPPMAN, WALTER 2007 *Public Opinion*. New York: NuVision [first published in 1922]
ROSS, KAREN 2009 *Gendered Media: Women, Men, and Identity Politics*, London: Rowman and Littlefield
SILVERSTONE, ROGER 1994 *Television and Everyday Life*, London: Routledge
—— 2007 *Media and Morality*, Cambridge: Polity Press
TUCHMAN, GAYE 1978 *Making News: A Study in the Construction of Reality*, New York: The Free Press

# Access denied: the anatomy of silence, immobilization and the gendered migrant

Katharine Sarikakis

**Abstract**
This article argues that the status of migrant subjects is characterized by a loss of communication rights and locates the instances where this loss is most visible. It investigates the process of silencing and immobilization of migrants and the particular forms it takes for female migrants through the disenablement of communicative acts. In this process the detained migrant loses her status as an interlocutor, irrespectively of the instances and processes that allow her–or demand of her–to speak. The state of exceptionality assigned to detained migrants is supported in the criminalization of migration laws and securitization, which together with widespread policies of incarceration in the West have become the anti-pode of the fundamental principles of free movement and expression. Silence and immobilization constitute the 'standard' rather than exceptional conditions of people on the move that shadow them across every step of their way, geographically, politically, culturally, legislatively, socially.

**Introduction**

Globalization has been accompanied by the narrative of freedom: for markets, flow of goods, services and capital; movement of ideas; from the boundaries of space and time, and identity. Globalization 'draws our enthusiasm because it helps us imagine interconnection, travel and sudden transformation. Yet it draws us inside its rhetoric until we take its claims for true descriptions' (Tsing 2001, p. 69). Communication, the indispensable element of globalization, has attained mythical dimensions for its impact on the human experience as one of liberation, self-determination and connection (Mosco 2004). However, the imagery of 'free movement' and 'connection' concerns only a small portion of humanity. The article aims to highlight some of the profound gaps in our thinking about communication, freedom and the silent majorities of migrants and to connect the broader context of *immobilization* of women migrants with the process of *silencing*. It argues that immobilization and silencing are two core rather than exceptional conditions for people who attempt to 'go elsewhere' that have accentuated consequences for women.

Epistemologically, the following discussion refers to women *in transit* who become *immobilized* through formal confinement in detention camps[1] or other restricting conditions.[2] I do not explore communication in relation to 'settled' diasporic, 'naturalized' or other groups with a level of legal entitlement of residency, although one could extrapolate some core elements of this discussion to these groups. Rather, I am interested in those 'failing' to gain *recognition*, those suspended in between worlds and without status. Female migrants'[3] experiences and knowledge as a subordinate class due to their position vis-à-vis institutionalized 'androcentric value patterns' (Fraser 2007) is determined by the international gender division of labour, institutional patriarchy and sexual violence. Gender 'intersects' with 'race', class and disability in the 'matrix of domination' accompanying women in transit. The process of transit is 'organized', at least analytically, around institutionally determined 'moments': *exit* from threatening spaces (death, rape, poverty), *'journey'*, arrival at a transit space (borders) and either *detention* (and ultimately *removal/ return to original start*) or more seldom *authorized entry* to 'destination'. This discussion begins by contextualizing communicative aims to personhood, citizenship and legitimacy. It then connects those to the international political economies of migration, control over and incarceration of human beings by highlighting spaces and moments in the process of immobilisation and silencing of the female migrant.

**Personhood, communication and citizenship**

'The abjection suffered in the camps horribly illustrates the threat of exclusion which weighs on all interlocution' (Lyotard 2002, p. 187).

The despair of which Lyotard speaks when referring to the Holocaust extinction camps is the fear and knowledge of exclusion, isolation, extermination and annihilation of the living being when her or his very existence is threatened. Through the denial of physical existence one is denied to be an interlocutor, to have an other partner in dialogue. Lyotard (1993, p. 147) asserts, in interlocution:

a drama is played out between *me* and *you*, it is the drama of authorisation. The question or assertion that we address to others is invariably coupled with an entreaty: Deliver me from my abandonment, allow me to belong among you.

To speak and to be heard is a fundamental communication act through which the subject can derive certain benefits that only speech can provide. These are, for one, legitimacy of existence, as a human being (at any given time in any given location). Speech-only derived benefits are withdrawn when silencing takes place–and this silencing does not have to preclude people from uttering words (Maitra 2009).

Silencing produces a wrong. Communicative disablement takes place when the speaker 'is unable to fully and successfully perform her intended communicative act' (Maitra 2009, p. 327) because her intended audience fails to satisfy her intentions either (a) that her audience recognizes that she has an informative intention or (b) that recognition of her intention gives her audience reason to respond to the content of her communication by fulfilling it (Maitra 2009). In the context of undocumented migration, one such instance is when women are not given the right to speak about their condition, and their words are not taken seriously, hence failing to produce a response by their intended audience (immigration officers or the police, for example). The wrong caused by silencing results in injury when women do not receive fair treatment. The ability to communicate and to be recognized as an interlocutor is at the heart of human rights and social justice, not only a functional right to seek and impart information. The more complex qualitative level of communicative act is lost for human beings not considered equal *others* to be granted the role of interlocutor. This is an overpowering position in which migrants find themselves when incarcerated and immobilized in modern-day camps. Below, I show that migrants' right to communicative acts is illegitimately and unilaterally disabled through material, legal, procedural and political economic constraints. This is more so for women on the move whose level of vulnerability is exacerbated due to gendered causes and consequences of migration.

The politics of inclusion and participation are inextricably linked to that of recognition and citizenship, whereby 'institutionalized patterns of cultural value recognize some categories of social actors as normative and others as deficient or inferior' (Fraser 2000, p. 114). Although communication rights–as fourth-generation and second-order rights–may seem secondary in confinement–a state of exceptionality–they constitute the testing ground of civil liberties for 'recognized' citizens. The notion of 'voice' and legitimacy is what underscores 'communication rights' as a system of human rights provisions, including freedom of expression, access to information, the right to education and literacy, freedom of assembly, right to free movement and the right to dignity. Although not recognized as a separate legal format of rights, the framework of the right to communicate is process oriented, securing other rights (McIver, Birdsall and Rasmussen 2003; Birdsall 2008; Hamelink and Hoffmann 2008).[4] Claims for the recognition of the 'right to communicate' do not consider migrants specifically. Nevertheless, communication is considered:

> a fundamental social process, a basic human need and a foundation of all social organizations. Everyone, everywhere, at any time should have the opportunity to participate in communication processes and no one should be excluded from their benefits. (Civil Society Declaration to the WSIS 2003)

My interest here is not to analyse the adequacy or otherwise of a universalistic communication rights claim, but rather to juxtapose its universal political claim about the recognition of personhood to the politics of women migrants' loss of this right. Not only the *legality* of speech but also the *legitimacy* of speech, and the *authority* to speak are the elements of a right to speak. For Lyotard (2002), there are three levels of this right: the faculty of interlocution, the legitimation of speech, whereby 'something other'–that which one knows not–is announced, and legitimacy of speech, 'the positive right to speak, which recognises in the citizen the right to address the citizen' (Lyotard 2002, p. 185). Hence, the (ideal) republic encourages everyone to speak and forbids the arbitrary deprivation of speech: 'It discourages terror' (Lyotard 2002, p. 186).

The governance of the conditions of speech and communicative act is situated within the context of the politics of globalization and the 'republic' and the ways in which it relates to 'outsiders'. Today it 'securitizes' heterogeneity, whereby difference–'that which one does not know'–becomes 'too visible'. Irregular migrants 'personify' that which is not the norm, that which is not known. The republic's response is to render them 'deficient or inferior', dehumanize them, negate them recognition as civic beings, exceptionalize and ultimately silence them. The 'state-of-emergency' discourse signals the abrupt break with normal politics, decision-making bypasses democratic processes and the citizen is symbolically annihilated. The mechanism of exemption undermines the public sphere and compromises political recognition (Sarikakis 2006). The violence of annihilation takes on an almost literal dimension when non-citizens are concerned: the extension of *social* rights to non-citizens is abruptly interrupted with the securitization of western politics and the criminalization of the migrant

(Arat-Koc 1999; Miller 2003; Picum 2007a, 2007b, 2009). Not only the 'polis' becomes an inaccessible communicative space for citizens, it also becomes dangerous to the outsider.

Illocutionary inclusion, being part of the 'polis', engaging in public speech, remains a core value of citizenship as in ancient Greece. Not only the core elements of participation in the political arena, as the dominant interpretation of the Athenian citizenship tells us, but other patterns of citizenship praxis become even more urgent in our era of global human mobilities. Not only men's role in the public domain, but also women's leadership in the family life, religion and social life of the 'polis' was recognized. Protection of the *citizen body* was a paramount element of citizenship extended to women through laws prohibiting physical assault, enslavement and punishment (Patterson 2009). The possibility for recognition and inclusion were inherent in laws enabling slaves to become free, and 'barbarians' 'affiliated' citizens, or *astoi*, with a share in the 'polis'. Today, some social and cultural dimensions of citizenship rights are by law required to be afforded to non-citizens, to enable them to maintain a sense of self-governance and on the basis of fundamental rights. International refugee and armed conflict law and human rights declarations[5] are juridical expressions of dimensions to protect the citizen body and safeguard the interlocutor. However, the state of exceptionality allows for hindering unwanted groups of people from moving and has subsequently constructed borders of extraordinary presence. Geographies of im/mobilization emerge through the concentration of immobilized persons, those who are related to migrants and in particular children, and the mobile disadvantaged classes (Sassen 2002; Yeoh and Lam 2007). Next, I explore the intersections and instances of physical and illocutionary immobilization.

## Women in the international political economy of migration

'Whether we are willing to debate seriously and pay attention to the conditions of people who are not citizens or voters is a test of this House [of Commons] and a test of our humanity' Abbott (2010).

The 'space for speech' in the context of recognition consists of two dimensions: that of the 'Other' as the ability and capacity to voice one's own condition, and the space occupied by voices of the 'norm' speaking of the 'Other'. In Athenian terms, this is the speech of the 'barbarian', which matters insofar its communication is received speech that is heard as well as spoken. Speech *about* the Other is determined by a system of factors, which have to do with the position of the 'Other' or 'barbarian' in relation to political economic structures of global migration, and hegemonic discourses in the immaterial, cultural realms of the 'normal' citizens. Non-/citizenship is determined by the nexus of international political economy and 'immigration renationalising politics' (Sassen 1996). Media panics and electoral campaigns' rhetoric[6] draw a picture of 'asylum seekers' and 'illegal' immigrants 'flooding'[7] the West, despite the fact that migration is in absolute terms low, with net migration in Europe 1.4 migrants per 1,000 annually in 2005, or 4.2 per 1,000 in North America (UN Population Division 2006).[8] Media and political discourses about immigration and asylum represent people in transit as a threat, but these concern only certain 'races' and classes of unwanted 'barbarians' (Roth 1998; Danso and McDonald 2001; Sjöberg and Ingegerd 2008).[9] Even so, only a small proportion of the world's refugees, 2 million out of 13.5 million, are actually located in the developed countries (UN Population Division 2006),[10] while in the last quarter of 2009 in the EU, a colossal 73 per cent of asylum applications were rejected (Eurostat 2010, p. 7). The rate of *rejection* of asylum applications for the UK and Austria was 78 per cent, France 86.5 per cent, Germany 68 per cent, Greece 98.6 per cent, and Spain 90 per cent. These numbers are of particular significance when considering the gendered causes and character of migration across three core dimensions of human flow: who travels (and why), where to, and under which socio-legal conditions? As Sudbury (2004, p. 155) argues, when writing about imprisonment and confinement of the African diaspora:

> questions of mobility—who travels, who cannot, who sets sail, who stays home, who can cross borders, who is detained behind them— are deeply gendered... these questions are also infused with the politics of class, citizenship and the social construction of criminality.

The *feminization of migration* is changing the face of human flow and is accompanied by an expanded reach of *silencing* practices. Although already by 1960 women made up 47 per cent of migrants (Zlonik 2003; INSTRAW 2007a) women now migrate not only as spouses and family members of male migrants but as workers in their own right. They are also refugees of ethnic wars, and seek protection for their children from abusive relationships, harmful customs, rape and violence in conflict zones (Refugee Council 2010), in addition to avoiding persecution due to their political or religious beliefs. The causes for female migration are not to be found only in crises in countries of origin, but equally in crises in destination countries, such as the 'care crisis' of the western world that requires the labour of domestic or medical carers in houses, hospices and hospitals (INSTRAW 2007b) or seasonal labour in the agricultural sector. Although the global North needs the labour of women, it controls their mobility and voice by withholding their social rights in feminized jobs in the informal economies of care. Global labour chains in care provision are based on the gender division of labour, reproduced across centres to the periphery (INSTRAW 2007b). Hence, the recipients of precarious and poorly remunerated jobs are most typically disadvantaged women migrants whose 'options' for the pursuit of a better life in the global labour market range largely between servitude, as domestics in wealthy nations, and prostitution, as sex 'entertainers' (Mies 1998; Pittaway and Bartolomei 2001; Ong 2008; Rubin et al. 2008).

Globally, migration geographies are largely feminized as women outnumber men in their effort to reach the 'developed' world: in Indonesia and Sri Lanka, 68 and 75 per cent of migrants are women, respectively. In the USA, a receiving country, documented migrants have been predominantly female since 1930 (Borak 2005). Contrary to media representations of migrants costing the economy, overall, non-EU migrants make a significant contribution to labour input in the EU, accounting for 6.7 per cent of the labour force on average, compared with their share of 6 per cent in the total adult population (European Commission 2008). Their contribution to the labour force exceeds 10 per cent in Austria, Cyprus, Estonia, Latvia and Spain (European Commission 2008). However, in many Member States, the integration of recent female immigrants appears particularly problematic, with employment rate gaps relative to EU-born women exceeding 25 percentage points in Austria, Belgium, Finland, France, the Netherlands and Sweden (European Commission 2008).

The colonies or modern-day peripheries *as well as* the centres in the global North are managed in the production–accumulation cycle through the global operation of patriarchy, accumulation and the international division of labour on the basis of a gender division of labour (Mies 1998). It is the subordination of the periphery that fuels specific production models in the centres, including the 'humanization' of western women's conditions who can escape menial, low-esteem and poorly remunerated (or unpaid) work, such as caring for the elderly or cleaning jobs, by employing women from the periphery. Mies (1998, p. 142) maintains that the process of 'housewifization', under which women in post-industrial societies are controlled, coerced or conditioned to roles of consumption, is accompanied by the simultaneous 'housewifization' of women from developing countries, meaning their treatment as invisible producers, their work seen as *activity* and only supplementary. When seeking entry to western countries women are not seen as highly skilled workers, especially if they enter under family immigration (Bach 2009). Worldwide, their numbers as highly skilled workers are lower than men's, while more highly skilled women are occupied in low-skilled jobs than men (Rubin et al. 2008). The occupations of most migrant women in the West are as personal and protective service workers, sales and services elementary occupations, office clerks, models, salespersons and demonstrators (Rubin et al. 2008), often under slave-like labour conditions and with a lack of social rights.[11]

## New borders and the anatomy of silence

The drama of authorization among interlocutors of which Lyotard (2002) speaks is visible when gender, race and class intersect. International law provides legitimacy, authorization for some and not others, as the journey of migration involves multiple levels of negotiation between the subjects who claim a right to interlocution and those who possess it: those who enter the new 'polis' and those who inhabit it (Pittaway and Bartolomei 2001). However, the law has in mind 'clean' narratives about those who seek to be heard, and complex matrices of domination cannot always be understood in practical and legal terms.

*Securitization and criminalization of immigration policies* in the global North (Miller 2003) has seen the integration of immigration law into criminal law, and the use of criminal law to deal with immigration challenges; the criminalization of the foreigner; the withdrawal of rights–economic, social, cultural–for migrants and those in detention; the increase in detention places; conflation of detention facilities with prisons and detention of irregular migrants in prisons; the introduction of the fast-track process for the deportation of applicants; and the use of military means to address requests for entry (Miller 2003; Fernández, Manavella and Ortuno 2009; Silveira Gorski, Fernández and Manavella 2009). Women and men are silenced by institutions through guards, the police and border officers. Women migrants are further silenced by ostensibly gender-blind international law, which fails to recognize their experience: only recently has rape been recognized as a war crime. Yet, no specific provision is made in cases of gender-based violence when handling asylum applications and women refugees are less likely to be granted full refugee status (Pittaway and Bartolomei 2001; Women Against Rape 2010). Culturally and institutionally, communication about sexual traumas in camps is often trivialized (Pittaway and Bartolomei 2001; Egharevba 2006). Speaking about sexual violence as part of a formal process becomes a form of torture for violence survivors, because their authority to speak is tested: a rejection of asylum application is a threat to their integrity *and* life. The confidential character of this communication is at odds with the context of interrogation, formality and demand to reduce complexity to names, dates, numbers and descriptions, repeatedly to one officer after another. To gain protection, the survivor is obliged to return to that from which she is escaping. 'Speaking' in the asylum interview context is not an act of interlocution in Lyotard's sense of citizen addressing citizen; *made* to speak under power relations is not a matter of free will or control over one's own personhood.

Volatile changes in the position of previously sender countries, such as the European peripheries of Greece, Italy or Spain, that have now become massive 'reception' centres for the whole of Europe have not been accompanied by material and social resources that would allow them to recognize a legitimate interlocutor in the face of 'barbarians'. As a response, 'foreigners camps' have sprung across Europe, and outside its borders, creating control zones to repel outsiders at the gates.[12] External camps mark the 'actual borders of the European Union: Morocco, Algeria, Ukraine' operate as 'European border watchdogs' (Migreurop 2009a). Periphery countries, such as Greece, function as the final 'frontier' for 'tidying up' the messy arrivals. Once 'deeper' in the EU (Germany, France, UK), migrants are immobilized in internal camps and then sent back to the first port of entry under the Dublin II agreement, even years after they have entered their destination. Europe immobilizes and silences its 'barbarians' to border zones and through indiscriminate expulsions (Migreurop 2009b).

A new map of borders and flow geographies emerges, based not on the migrant journey but on the processes of immobilization and silencing. Communication acts, self-governance and speech are the first victims in a long list of revoked rights as interlocution becomes de facto a site of constant struggle through territories of strange languages, systems, cultural and legal codes, and danger. This a journey haunted by *silence*:

> Because you have prepared mentally for the journey, it is hard and dangerous, and you hope that this time you will get through. But when [the police] catch you, you just collapse. You are depressed. If you start shouting as well, if you try to say something, they hit you. You know, we don't even ask them for some respect, but if they also hit you, you know.... You don't have the right to speak to them, nor the right to ask to go to hospital. If you do so, if you talk to them, they beat you. (Interview 2008 in Migreurop 2009b).

In these conditions, to know one's rights is paramount. Civil society organizations demand that asylum applicants are clearly informed of their various rights for information, representation and interpreters of the same gender (Asylum Aid 2007). However, 19 per cent of UK detainees had no access to legal assistance at the time of their interview (Bail for Immigration Detainees 2009). Immobilized women's capacity to change their status depends on use of their speech rights. In order for their social rights to be 'returned', it is necessary that communication processes and channels are open and enabling:

I am scared that I am becoming invisible and no-one knows I am here. I feel quite suicidal and only the thought of Fi keeps me going. It is shocking and very emotionally draining to be locked in the system, and locked up with your tools of communication taken away or blunted. (interview in Ross 2008).

The operation of the camps takes place away from public scrutiny: there is little access to camps and detainees for non-governmental organizations, journalists or other organizations (Brothers 2007; Migreurop 2009b).[13] As camps are often under the control of private companies, their contractual obligations, expectations and infrastructure affect the ways in which decisions are being made on a day-to-day basis at border control points (Weber and Gelsthorpe 2000; Bacon 2005). Additionally, laws of commercial confidentially do not allow the full spectrum of data on camps to become public. The consequences are manifold: migrants are being multiply silenced as they are kept away from public debate, their contacts to the outside world severed, their condition untold. Their non-existence status, as non-authorized speaking subjects, normalizes further their silencing under exceptionality.

The political economy of migration extends to the internal organizations of new borderlands. Their profits derive from contracts with the state, their financing by the public through taxation. They also derive from 'work' schemes for detainees whose pay lags behind the national minimum wage (Women Against Rape 2010); understaffing and substandard services, such as food below expected standards[14] (Bacon 2005; Taylor and Cooper 2002). The criminalization of irregular migrants 'delegitimizes' one's personhood: the citizen body is not protected; participation in the 'polis' is disabled; the speaker is silenced:

> ...our minds have been lock and our hands cut off because we can't express anything fully about our cases. We do not have any approach to emails. We can't discuss anything with anybody as we are detained and telephones are much expensive which we can't afford. We are all going to be refused and there is no choice whether you have evidence or not because they are saying these documents are fake and not genuine (Cutler 2007, p. 2; see also: Bail for Immigration Detainees 2007, Bail for Immigration Detainees 2009).

Often, the ultimate act of speech is one that entails the ultimate act of refusal to speak, the risk of death: women have gone on hunger strikes, such as in the UK Yarl's Wood detention centre, in order to draw attention to their condition and have their voices heard (Silove, Steel and Mollica 2001; Brothers 2007; Migrants' Rights Centre Ireland

2008; Travis 2009). Abjection and exclusion are materially manifested: without a safe physical and symbolic (communicative) space within which experiences, political claims and expectations are expressed, connecting with others is nearly impossible. Hence, a form of universality of fundamental freedoms for humanity must aim at the empowerment of marginalized groups in public discourse (Hansen 2009) without minoritizing, trivializing or relativizing women's voices. civil society organizations and migrants know it all too well; an effort to create the space for interlocution proves to be an indispensable political tool:

> The Women's group is a crucial opportunity for our clients to have a voice within a system that renders them powerless, and a safe space in which to share their experiences, concerns and ideas. This has included contributing to focus groups to influence the Home Office and the Department of Health. (Refugee Council 2010, p. 4)

In the silence and immobilization nexus, basic rights are systematically revoked (Silove, Steel and Mollica 2001; Miller 2003; Oberoi 2009); in many cases, the basic right to life is 'revoked'.[15] The 'polis' is 'cancelled' for those waiting in camps, the 'territory of exemption' (Fassin 2002, p. 228). Lack of public scrutiny and debate imposes silence on the experience and testimonies of thousands of 'people who simply want to go elsewhere' (Migreurop 2009b, p. 34). Moreover, when the 'barbarian' Other enters the public arena she is confronted with racist, xenophobic discourses, stereotypical (mis)representations (Van Dijk 1993; Ross 2000; Spoonley and Butcher 2009) that serve to undermine equal interlocution.

**Concluding remarks**

The world, while 'experientially shrinking', becomes claustrophobic for the immobilized and silenced migrant. Within the western political systems, the values of personal liberty, freedom of expression, equality before law and humanism are put to the test: to which degree do these values and rights apply to the Other? To what extent does the Other become a case of exemption from democratic processes and ceases to be the 'other than me' of interlocution? How does the confinement of people seeking to 'go elsewhere' reconcile with claims of world openness and interconnection? Today, the migrant subjects criminalised by punitive nation-state border agencies and removal centres, while the media and political discourse adopt 'practices and priorities of the criminal justice system' (Miller 2003, p. 613). The triangle of dehumanization consists of the privatization of the incarceration system, instrumental in the expansion of detention spaces; the criminalization of the migrant and development of punitive migration laws with the core aim to expel (Silveira Gorski, Fernández and Manavella 2009); and the gendered construction of normative standards of international law. The capability for communication is an indispensable part of personhood, however the legal frameworks protecting the person are undermined by policies of exemption and exclusion. It is precisely under these conditions that the right to speak, with authority, and be heard, is more important than ever.

Integral to the negotiation process of migratory experience is the relation of the subject to the means of symbolic existence, the range of possibilities for the finding and articulation of one's voice in cultural, political and legal terms. In law, this articulation is understood as the enjoyment of human rights, not only civil and political but also economic, social and cultural rights. Protests in detention camps come to remind us of our civic duty to recognize the human in those immobilized others. Women detainees hunger striking in UK's Yarl's Wood or sewing their lips with wire in Samos in Greece mobilize the non-citizen body so that it is recognized; sacrifice the body for its survival; silence themselves for the right to speak. They make the most powerful statement about the state of the republic. Speech as an element of the 'polis' requires to be legally and materially available to all voices or, as Lyotard (2002, p 187) argues 'the effort of translation must be endlessly renewed'. In the condition of 'emergency' and segregation of people into dehumanized invaders and legal citizens, being 'part of the polis' is the ultimate test of legitimacy for the republic itself.

## Acknowledgements

The author would like to acknowledge the helpful comments of two anonymous referees and the guest editor Dr Myria Georgiou. Also thanks to Dimitris Tsapogas for support with some of the article's data.

## Notes

1. The article understands 'camps' to include locations that although 'open', inhibit movement due to conditions imposed on people (http://www.migreurop.org).
2. Human trafficking is most relevant in exemplifying the multiple manifestations of immobilization, exploitation and silencing of women and children and a major factor in migration. Indeed the whole article could have been written around this particular phenomenon and I thank an anonymous reviewer for suggesting its mention. In this discussion I concentrate on the contexts determined by formal, otherwise 'legitimate' and legal actors, such as states, policy makers, police, detention centre companies, border and immigration officers. All these actors are less than understanding or adequately sensitized to

deal with the social and individual harm and injustice on women caught in human trafficking.
3. This paper understands 'migrant' to be anyone who crosses borders, although invariably the discussion focuses on unwanted migrants. This usually means migrants from third conflict or poverty-ridden countries, although depending on national contexts even 'less' foreigners (such as inner European migrants) are treated as unwanted.
4. To this conclusion came d'Arcy (1969) in his article criticizing governments for concentrating on content instead of the process of communication. Although not clearly defined, the 'right to communicate' relates to the comprehensive material and symbolic availability of the means through which communication can take place. It put forth a claim to a more just world order in the 1970s and 1980s with the MacBride Report and the New World Information and Communication Order. The debate resurfaced during the World Summit of the Information Society (WSIS). Despite global grass roots and UNESCO support, the proposals for a specific provision were not included in the final declarations (Chakravartty and Sarikakis 2006; Hamelink and Hoffmann 2008).
5. For example, International Humanitarian Law, 1951 Refugee Convention, also see the UN refugee Agency (http://www.unhcr.org/cgi-bin/texis/vtx/home) etc.
6. In the UK 2010 electoral campaigns, the party leaders' debates very quickly turned to the 'need' to control immigration. Even the Liberal Democrats, whose political manifesto included the proposal to allow immigrants to live in the community instead of detention centres, retreated when faced with populist xenophobic discourses (see Flynn 2010; Grayson 2010; Kikrup 2010).
7. In Europe, increase in immigration has slowed; some countries (including Germany, Austria and the Netherlands) have seen a reduction in migration (Eurostat 2008).
8. Overall, global migration has increased by just 0.5 per cent since the 1960s (INSTRAW 2007; UN Population Division 2006).
9. Public discourse focuses on third countries' migration to Europe. However, British and German immigrants to EU countries are second only to Polish and Romanian immigrants according to Eurostat: nearly half of British citizen migrants went to Spain in 2006, while Australian (26,000) and South African citizens (16,000) in the same year were among the top five citizenships migrating to Britain (Eurostat 2008).
10. Asylum applications have fallen from 483,000 in 1990 to 282,000 in 2004 in the EU (Eurostat 2006).
11. The sex trade is a core source of illegal immigration and slave labour: the UN estimates that up to 600,000 women are brought to Europe illegally every year, with 80 per cent of them absorbed in the sex industry (Rubin et al. 2008).
12. On the political economic relations of extra-territorial camps, their politics, data and geographies (http://www.migreurope.org).
13. Even the Office of the United Nations High Commissioner for Refugees (UNHCR) is often not allowed access to camps or is presented with distorted pictures of life in camps (Brothers 2007).
14. See Taylor and Cooper 2002 for an extensive report on privatization of correctional facilities and the level of service to inmates. Also see 'Privatisation of Parklea. Analysis of the potential Operators. July 2009' (http://www.docstoc.com/docs/31829609/Private-Prisons-%E2%80%93-Company-Profiles) and 'Private detention centres reap mammoth profits' (http://www.abc.net.au/pm/stories/s215963.htm). Seven out of ten detention centres in the UK are managed by Global Solutions Ltd, a company involved in education, investment and prisons. Other private companies involved in the UK correctional system, the most privatized in Europe, are Wackenhut Corrections and Serco. See the report by Corporate Watch (http://www.corporatewatch.org.uk/?lid = 1838) and civil society organizations such as no-lager (http://www.nolager.org).
15. On the conditions of existence–and extermination–of refugees and 'illegal' immigrants, see the detailed report of Migreurop (2009b).

## References

ABBOTT, DIANE 2010 'Parliamentary debate on Yarl's Wood Detention Centre', 11 February. Available from: http://www.dianeabbott.org.uk/news/speeches/news.aspx? p = 102575 [Accessed 10 October 2011]
ARAT-KOC, SEDEF 1999 'Neo-liberalism, state restructuring and immigration: changes in Canadian policies in the 1990s', *Journal of Canadian Studies*, vol. 34, no. 2, pp. 31–56
ASYLUM AID 2007 *Asylum is not Gender Neutral: Protecting Women Seeking Asylum*, London: Asylum Aid. Available from: http://www.asylumaid.org.uk/data/files/publications/70/Asylum_is_not_gender_neutral.pdf [Accessed 10 October 2011]
BACH, AMANDINE 2009 'Reframing immigration, integration and asylum policies from a gender perspective: ensuring gender-fair policies', *European Social Watch Report: Migrants in Europe as Development Actors*. Available from: http://www.socialwatch.eu/wcm/gender_perspective.html#footnote-1323-5-backlink
BACON, CHRISTINE 2005 *The evolution of immigration detention in the UK: The involvement of private prison companies*. Refugee Studies Centre Working Paper no. 27, http://www.rsc.ox.ac.uk/PDFs/RSCworkingpaper27.pdf, Oxford: University of Oxford
BAIL FOR IMMIGRATION DETAINEES 2009 *Out of Sight, Out of Mind: Experiences of Immigration Detention in the UK*, London: Bail for Immigration Detainees
BIRDSALL, WILLIAM F. 2008 "Constructing a right to communicate: the UN Declaration on the Rights of Indigenous Peoples", *Global Media Journal*, vol. 7, no. 13
BORAK, JILL 2005 'Women migrant workers: embracing empowerment over victimization', paper presented at When Women Gain, So Does the World, IWPR's Eighth International Women's Policy Research Conference, June, Washington
BROTHERS, CAROLINE 2007 'Obscurity and confinement for migrants in Europe', *The New York Times*, 30 December
CIVIL SOCIETY DECLARATION TO THE WSIS 2003 *Shaping Information Societies for Human Needs*. http://www.itu.int/wsis/docs/geneva/civil-society-declaration.pdf [accessed May 3 2009]
D'ARCY, JEAN 1969 'Direct broadcast satellites and the right to communicate', *EBU Review*, vol. 118, pp. 14–8
DANSO, RANSFORD and MCDONALD, DAVID A. 2001 'Writing xenophobia: immigration and the print media in post-apartheid South Africa', *Africa Today*, vol. 48, no. 3, pp. 115–37
EUROPEAN COMMISSION 2008 *Employment in Europe 2008*, Luxembourg: European Commission
EUROSTAT, 2006 *Populations Statistics*, Luxembourg: European Communities
―――― 2008 *Population and Social Conditions 98/2008*, Luxembourg: European Communities
―――― 2010 *Data in Focus: Asylum Applicants and First Instance Decisions on Asylum Applications in Q4 2009 18/2010*. Available from: http://epp.eurostat.ec.europa.eu/cache/ity_offpub/ks-qa-10-018/en/ks-qa-10-018-en.pdf [Accessed 10 October 2011]
FRASER, NANCY 2000 'Rethinking recognition', *New Left Review*, no. 3, pp. 107–20
FRASER, NANCY 2007 'Feminist politics in the age of recognition: a two-dimensional approach to gender justice", *Studies in Social Justice*, vol. 1, no. 1, pp. 23–35
FERNÁNDEZ, CRISTINA, MANAVELLA, ALEJANDRA and ORTUNO, JOSE MARIA 2009 *The Effects of Exceptional Legislation on Criminalization of Immigrants and People Suspected of Terrorism*, Barcelona: University of Barcelona. Available from: http://www.libertysecurity.org/IMG/pdf_FINAL-_The_effects_of_exceptional_legislation_on_the_criminalization_of_migrants_and_people_suspected_of_terrorism.pdf [Accessed 10 October 2011]
FLYNN, DON 2010 'Immigration and the general election: did the dog bark, or didn't it?', Migrants Rights Network. Available from: http://www.migrantsrights.org.uk/blog/2010/05/immigration-and-general-election-did-dog-bark [Accessed 10 October 2011]

GRAYSON, JOHN 2010 'Reflections on the media, immigration and the election', Institute of Race Relations. Available from: http://www.irr.org.uk/2010/may/ha000020.html [Accessed 10 October 2011]
HAMELINK, CEES J. and HOFFMAN, JULIA 2008 "The state of the right to communicate", *Global Media Journal*, vol. 7, no. 13,
HANSEN, RANDALL 2009 'The poverty of postnationalism: citizenship, immigration, and the new Europe', *Theory and Society*, vol. 38, no. 1, pp. 1–24
INSTRAW, 2007a *Feminisation of Migration. Gender, Remittances and Development, Working Paper 1*, Geneva: United Nations
―――― 2007b *Global Care Chains. Gender, Remittances and Development, Working Paper 2*, Geneva: United Nations
KIKRUP, JAMES 2010 'General Election 2010: Nick Clegg gets immigration figures "wrong" in final television debate', *Daily Telegraph*, 30 April. Available from: http://www.telegraph.co.uk/news/election-2010/7654278/General-Election-2010-Nick-Clegg-gets-immigration-figures-wrong-in-final-television-debate.html [Accessed 10 October 2011]
LYOTARD, JEAN-FRANCOIS 2002 "The other's rights", in The Belgrade Circle (ed.), *The Politics of Human Rights*, New York: Verso
MAITRA, ISHANI 2009 'Silencing speech', *Canadian Journal of Philosophy*, vol. 39, no. 2, pp. 309–38
MCIVER, WILLIAM J. JR., BIRDSALL, WILLIAM F. and RASMUSSEN, MERRILEE 2003 'The Internet and the right to communicate' *First Monday*, vol. 8, no. 12. Available from: http://firstmonday.org/htbin/cgiwrap/bin/ojs/index.php/fm/article/view/1102/1022 [Accessed 10 October 2011]
MIES, MARIA 1998 *Patriarchy and accumulation on a world scale: women in the international division of labour*, Basingstoke: MacMillan
MIGREUROP, 2009a *Atlas des migrants en Europe. Geographie critique des politiques migratoires*, Paris: Armand-Colin
―――― 2009b *Europe's Murderous Borders*, Paris: Migeurop. Available from: http://www.migreurop.org/IMG/pdf/Rapport-Migreurop-nov2009-en-final.pdf [Accessed 10 October 2011]
MILLER, TERESA A. 2003 'Citizenship and severity: recent immigration reforms and the new penology', *Georgetown Immigration Law Journal*, vol. 17, pp. 611–6.
MOSCO, VINCENT 2004 *The digital sublime: myth, power, and cyberspace*, Cambridge, Mass: MIT Press
MIGRANTS' RIGHTS CENTRE IRELAND 2008 *Life in the Shadows: An Exploration of Irregular Migration in Ireland*, Dublin: Migrants' Rights Centre Ireland
OBEROI, PIA 2009 'Defending the weakest: the role of international human rights mechanisms in protecting the economic, social and cultural rights of migrants', *International Journal on Multicultural Societies*, vol. 11, no. 1, pp. 19–35
ONG, AIWHA 2008 'A bio-cartography: maids, neo-slavery and NGOs', in Sheila Benhabib and Judith Resnik (eds), *Migrations and Mobilities. Citizenship, Borders, and Gender*, New York: New York University Press
PATTERSON, C.B. 2009 'Gender and Citizenship in the Ancient World', in Seyla Benhabib and Judith Resnik (eds), *Migrations and Mobilities: Citizenship, Borders, and Gender*, New York: NYU Press
PICUM, 2007a *Undocumented Migrants Have Rights! An Overview of the International Human Rights Framework*, Brussels: Picum
―――― 2007b *Access to Healthcare for Undocumented Migrants in Europe*, Brussels: PICUM
―――― 2009 *Undocumented Children in Europe: Invisible Victims of Immigration Restrictions*, Brussels: PICUM
PITTAWAY, EILEEN and BARTOLOMEI, LINDA 2001 'The multiple discrimination against refugee women', *Refuge*, vol. 19, no. 6, pp. 21–32

REFUGEE COUNCIL 2010 *Rape and Sexual Violence: The Experiences of Refugee Women in the UK*, London: British Refugee Council. Available from: http://www.refugeecouncil.org.uk/Resources/Refugee%20Council/downloads/Refugee%20women%20briefing%20March%202010.pdf [Accessed 10 October 2011]
ROSS, KAREN 2000 'In whose image? TV criticism and black minority views', in Simon Cottle (ed.), *Ethnic Minorities and the Media. Changing Cultural Boundaries*, Buckingham: Open University Press
ROSS, SHAN 2008 'Why this woman's story shames Scotland', *The Scotsman*, 3 June. Available from: http://thescotsman.scotsman.com/latestnews/-Why-this-woman39s-story.4143684.jp [Accessed 10 October 2011]
ROTH, LORNA 1998 "The delicate acts of "colour balancing": multiculturalism and Canadian television broadcasting policies and practices", *Canadian Journal of Communication*, vol. 23, no. 4
RUBIN, JENNIFER et al. 2008 *Migrant Women in the European Labour Force: Current Situation and Future Prospects*, Santa Monica, CA: RAND Corporation. Available from: http://www.rand.org/pubs/technical_reports/TR591 [Accessed 10 October 2011]
SARIKAKIS, KATHARINE 2006 *Making Security: Citizenship, Public Sphere and the Condition of Symbolic Annihilation*, http://www.libertysecurity.org/article1208.html [Accessed 10 January 2011]
SASSEN, SASKIA 1996 *Losing Control? Sovereignty in an Age of Globalization*, New York: Columbia University Press
—— 2002 'Is this the way to go? Handling immigration in a global era', *Stanford Agora: An Online Journal of Legal Perspectives*, vol. 4
SILOVE, DERRICK, STEEL, ZACHARY and MOLLICA, RICHARD F. 2001 'Detention of asylum seekers: assault on health, human rights, and social development', *Lancet*, vol. 357, pp. 1436–37
SILVEIRA GORSKI, HÉCTOR C., FERNÁNDEZ, CRISTINA and MANAVELLA, ALEJANDRA 2009 *A Right-Based Approach to Migration Policies in a Context of Emergencies: 'Expelling States' and Semi-Persons in the European Union*. Barcelona: University of Barcelona. Available from: http://www.libertysecurity.org/IMG/pdf_deliverable_dic_2008.pdf [Accessed 10 October 2011]
SPOONLEY, PAUL and BUTCHER, ANDREW 2009 'Reporting superdiversity: the mass media and immigration in New Zealand', *Journal of Intercultural Studies*, vol. 30, no. 4, pp. 355–72
SUDBURY, JULIA 2004 'From the point of no return to the women's prison: writing contemporary spaces of confinement into diaspora studies', *Canadian Woman Studies*, vol. 23, no. 2, pp. 154–63
TAYLOR, PHIL and COOPER, CHRISTINE 2002 *Privatised Prisons and Detention Centres in Scotland: An Independent Report*. Available from: http://visar.csustan.edu/aaba/Cooper&Taylor.pdf [Accessed 10 October 2011]
TRAVIS, ALAN 2009 'Detention centre branded "unacceptable" for women and children', *Guardian*, 18 December. Available from: http://www.guardian.co.uk/uk/2009/dec/18/tinsley-detention-centre-unacceptable-children [Accessed 10 October 2011]
TSING, ANNA 2001 *The global situation*. In: Inda, Jonathan Xavier. Rosaldo, Renato (Hg.): The anthropology of globalization. A reader
UN POPULATION DIVISION 2006 *International Migration 2006*, New York: UN. Available from: http://www.un.org/esa/population/publications/2006Migration_Chart/Migration2006.pdf [Accessed 10 October 2011]
VAN DIJK, TEUN 1993 *Elite Discourse and Racism*, London: Sage
WEBER, L. and GELSTHORPE, L. 2000 *Deciding to detain: How decisions to detain asylum seekers are made at ports of entry*, Institute of Criminology: University of Cambridge
WOMEN AGAINST RAPE 2010 *Women speak out in Parliament against detention, deportation, privatisation and profiteering 14 January 2010*, London: Women Against Rape.

Available from: http://www.womenagainstrape.net/content/women-speak-out-parliament-against-detention-depor# [Accessed 10 October 2011]

YEOH, BRENDA S. A. and LAM, THEODORA 2007 "The costs of (im)mobility: children left behind and children who migrate with a parent", in Un Escap (ed.), *Perspectives on Gender and Migration*, New York: Un Escap Secretariat

ZLONIK, HANIA 2003 *The Global Dimensions of Female Migration*, Washington, DC: Migration Policy Institute. Available from: http://www.migrationinformation.org/Feature/display.cfm?ID = 109 [Accessed 10 October 2011]

# Getting integration right? Media transnationalism and *domopolitics* in Ireland

Gavan Titley

**Abstract**

This article examines the transnational media environments and experiences of Nigerian and Chinese nationals living in Ireland. It theorizes empirical research in the context of the mode of integration governance developed in the Republic of Ireland during a period of significant in-migration. Building on a theory of domopolitics, it suggests that Ireland's short-lived integration regime deployed culture and interculturalism as resources for the self-governing integration of all foreign nationals, while developing a system of civic stratification designed to limit claims to citizenship and social and economic rights. It examines the concomitant development of public service media policies in this context. Drawing on recent discussions of contrapuntal media readings, the article argues that transnational media experience refracts the lived tensions inherent in the disjuncture between the possibilities of cultural participation and the constraints of socio-political containment.

**Introduction**

This article examines the transnational media practices of Nigerian and Chinese discussants during a period characterized by an Irish governmental focus on integration, a focus replicated and adapted in the 'intercultural policies' adopted by the public service broadcaster, RTÉ. As non-EU citizens with residence permitted through a variety of channels – work permits, student visas, refugee status or with 'leave to remain' – they have been the imagined subjects of a politics that proposes integration as a primarily cultural 'two-way process' of undifferentiated majority/ minority relations, while living within a system of civic stratification based on a tiered legitimacy of labour utility and perceived impacts on social cohesion (Fanning 2009). The disconnect between culturalized narratives of integration, and restricted access to permanent status and economic and social rights, is primarily explored through the experiences of female discussants, who may be 'triply disadvantaged' in Ireland through gender inequality, racial discrimination and the precariousness of migrants in the labour market (Pillinger 2007).

As Eleonore Kofman summarizes, in western Europe '...immigration policies are directed towards selecting those who will be most advantageous to the economy, will fit into a pre-existing national culture, and not disrupt a supposed social and community cohesion' (2005, p. 463). The practices of the state in Ireland are congruent with this, while being mediated through 'soft' discourses of interculturalism and integration, as opposed to the variegated 'neo-assimilationist' agendas more commonly found in neighbouring countries (ibid. Fekete 2009). Media research provides an interesting space for examining the relationship between the structuration and culturalization of legitimate migrant presence. Given, as Roger Silverstone argues, that the primary cultural role of media work is 'boundary work', '...the endless, endless, endless, playing with difference and sameness' (2007, p. 19), public service media in Europe have been charged with and have adopted ambivalent roles in relation to the contemporary governance prerogative of integration. Media work is not only institutional, it is also the work of situated sense-making. For migrants, this involves working with the multiplicities of media in contexts of constraint, imbalances of power, and where boundaries are made and re-made in relation to their identities and presence. Silverstone posits a theory of such media work as the *contrapuntal*; empirically, as situated in a diverse yet transnationally convergent 'single media environment', but also experientially – as the inescapability of the presence of others, of a dialectic between presence and absence, of situatedness and dispersion (2007, pp. 84–7). Following a discussion of institutional integration discourse in the Republic of Ireland in relation to 'domopolitics' (Walters 2004), the article presents a thematic analysis of empirical research conducted as part of a 2007–9 research project examining migration, and media policy and practices. The analysis examines how mediated resources are incorporated into the constraints, situated affectivities and future orientations of young Chinese women working in Dublin, and Nigerian women and men of varying statuses reflecting, through media practices, on their future in a 'home' unsettled by racialization. Contrapuntal media practices integrate Irish and transnational media, providing resources for reflecting on and re-shaping relations of 'here' and 'there'. Yet discussants also reflected, through mediated resources, on the disjuncture between the constraints of status, and their experiences and modalities of integration. These practices elaborate the resistant social fact, as articulated by Ghassan Hage, that 'cultural integration' happens: often regardless of particular state policies, and in ways that exceed, evade, and undermine the majoritarian projections of those modes of governance (2000, pp. 238–40).

## Situating the politics of integration in Ireland

*Integration as 'domopolitics'*

Integration regimes in western Europe display an apparent contradiction between the expansion of stratifying systems of entry, status and residence, and the extensive formal and symbolic demands for loyalty and elective homogeneity made on migrants with these variegated legal statuses. The 'neo-assimilationist agendas' that now seek to protect social cohesion through demands for cultural affirmation were generated by the complex of migratory pressures experienced in western Europe in the post-Cold War period (Kofman 2005). These agendas, as Kofman argues, are integral to 'managed migration regimes' and processes of civic stratification: differentiated access to civil, economic and social rights, as well as potential citizenship, is organized according to the gradiated utility of migrant labour and concomitant modes of entry, employment and residence. In regulating the productive contribution of migrant labour and the manifold risks associated with migrants as 'social enemies' (Tsoukala 2005), integration governance produces differentiated modes of legal subjectification detached from processes of citizenship, while delineating acceptable ranges of possible conduct based on a projection of the idealized national citizen (McGhee 2008; Fekete 2009).

As Bryan Fanning details – in reflecting on the 2004 Citizenship Referendum that removed the birthright of citizenship from children of 'non-nationals' – the state in Ireland has developed a broadly similar structure. The incorporation of citizenship as a 'mechanism of civic stratification' is part of a structure of '...gradations of rights between citizens and non-citizens, immigrant "guest" workers, "illegal" workers, refugees and asylum-seekers...in which groups of people are differentiated by the legitimate claims they can make on the state' (Fanning 2009, p. 111). Prior to 2002, integration governance was restricted to those granted refugee status and labour migration was regarded as temporary (Boucher 2008, p. 22). In advance of the 2004 accession of new EU member states, Irish policy shifted to develop a system of stratification based on satisfying low-skilled labour needs from mobile EU labour, and a 'managed system' involving Green Cards and enhanced residence pathways for skilled non-EU labour (ibid). The economic recession since 2008 has provided significant evidence of the structured inequality and exploitation facilitated by the employer-held work permit system. The state response has been to ignore and enhance these restrictions, based, as a 2010 Migrant Rights Centre report contended,

> ...on a misunderstanding of migrant workers and their families as temporary residents whose position is entirely dependent on economic circumstances. Migrant workers and their families are thus actively encouraged to leave Ireland, or not to come here in the first place' (Crowley 2010, p. 5).

However, the gaps between 'nationals' and 'non-nationals' can be understood less as 'misunderstandings' than as systemic priorities, and integral to the project of integration governance in '...systems that couple security and migration with visions of integration' (Maguire and Murphy 2009, p. 3). Integration governance in Ireland may be interpreted as an iteration of what William Walters terms 'domopolitics' – a themed, securitized politics of home. In a configuration particularly suited to theorizing the 'neoliberalisation of Irish society' (Kirby, Ging and Cronin 2009, p. 205), Walters argues that the image of a coherent national economic system '...linked in turn to a social order...in an international order populated by discrete, bounded socio-economic systems engaged in mutual relations of trade' (2004, p. 244) has been largely replaced by configurations of the neoliberal state located in a space of flows, where the 'business' of governance involves tapping into and directing productive mobile goods. In this porous order, 'insecure societies' are held to be vulnerable to mobile 'bads', including such human mobilities as 'unskilled' workers and the delegitimized mobility of asylum-seeking.

Domopolitic cannot seek to arrest mobility, it looks to manage and discipline its costs and risks. It regulates suitable entry. Guests must learn the house rules – a common metaphor in integration debates – and submit to cultural governance. Home must be protected because its '...contents (our property) are valuable and envied by others' (2004, p. 241), implying guest self-sufficiency. Guests should not steal; the threat of the 'immigrant' is a threat to the residual welfare state, and domopolitics transfers (social) security to the policing of resource threats in a field of internal and transnational security, juxtaposing '...the "warm words" of community, trust and citizenship with the danger words of a chaotic outside – illegals, traffickers, terrorists' (Connolly 1995, p. 142). In Ireland as elsewhere, 'integration' is detached from a process of access to national citizenship through naturalization, and has become a border practice, beyond and inside the territorial border (Guild, Groenendijk and Carrera 2009, p. 15–17).

In a study of the 'feminisation of migration' to Ireland, Jane Pillinger (2007) illustrates how this mode of domopolitical governance specifically impacts on migrant women. While describing a diversity of experiences – and a recurrent reflection among her respondents that migration had increased some forms of autonomy and impacted on prevailing, dominant gender relations – Pillinger's research shows the divergence between the integration strategies and experiences of many migrant women and the legal-structural barriers they face. Difficulties in accessing social and economic rights to information, health services, childcare and maternity benefits are structured by limited access to secure status, independent status (for the spouses of employment permit-holders), rights to family reunification, and the disruption of mobile networks of care and support through visa regimes (Pillinger 2007, pp. 35–50). The domopolitical emphasis on policing the threat of the immigrant is further secured through a gendered rendition of civic stratification.

*Culture, governance and the integration narrative*

Western European integration politics is mediated through idioms conveying threatened and desired states of integration: *laïcité* in France, 'community cohesion' in the UK, 'standards and values' in the Netherlands, '*Leitkultur*' in Germany (Fekete 2009, pp. 62–3). These resurgent imaginaries cannot be understood without reference to the contemporary license provided by the rejection of a 'failed experiment' in multiculturalism. Regardless of the conceptual elasticity and contextual variations barely contained by the idea (Fleras 2009), multiculturalism has been inflated beyond the scope of empirical rebuttal, and provides a reductive, mobilizing metaphor for the manifold threats of difference to social cohesion and national unity (Vertovec and Wessendorf 2009; Lentin and Titley 2011).

Demands for conformity to national ideals are less pronounced in Ireland, where the mediation of a 'progressive multicultural image' is crucial to the globalized, foreign direct investment-dependent economy (Kirby et al. 2002, p. 197). Instead, integration governance was themed as 'a chance to get it right', a temporal emphasis that envisioned engaging with the problematic of migration just as other European countries transcended 'multiculturalism'. Influenced by the non-binding common principles at EU level (2004) the 2008 policy statement of the Office of a Minister of State for Integration (OMI) narrates 'experience in other countries' as shifting from 'relatively laissez-faire...to compulsory engagement'. This suggests that '...from Ireland's point of view, we may be able to position ourselves on a more advanced cycle rather than go through earlier cycles' (OMI 2008, pp. 35–6).

For all this modular precision, research consistently critiqued the lack of coherence in '...a collection of policy statements and piece-meal, reactive policy responses to immediate, experiential policy problems' (Boucher 2008, p. 6). Following the abolition and 'down-scaling' of agencies deemed central to integration[1] in an emergency budget in 2008, it becomes possible to theorize this piece-meal development as an aspect of what Christian Salmon terms 'narrative as instrument of control' (2010, pp. 6–10). Ireland's post-multicultural certainties were entirely discursive. 'Multiculturalism', for instance, was merely re-branded as 'interculturalism', a shift that extends a multiculturalist ontology of 'already there' cultures. This elided experiences of racism, while limiting more materialist forms of anti-racist politics (Lentin and McVeigh 2006).

Ireland exemplifies how, under domopolitics, the assertion of '...home as our place, where we belong, naturally, and where others, by definition, do not' (Walters 2004, p. 241) does not always depend on overt appeals to national homogeneity. Instead, culturalization delimits the political field while promoting culture as a managerial 'resource' (Yúdice 2003). For all the anxieties concerning futures of multiculturalist dis-cohesion, integration was not meaningfully re-garded as a question for social policy, as domopolitics works to manage cultural and economic threats in the absence of the social. Immigration policy acts as an integration filter selecting those deemed capable of economic self-sufficiency (Boucher 2008) and integration discourse attempts to cultivate '...self-sufficient and autonomous immigrants, who must work on themselves in order to be independent, and committed to contributing to the Irish economy and society, in order that they may be integrated' (Gray 2006, p. 130).

*The boundary work of media institutions*

If integration provides a cultural control narrative, it also provides a legitimation narrative for national broadcasters de-centred by digitalization, media transnationalization, and audience fragmentation (Larsen 2010). In Roger Silverstone's theorization of *media work as boundary work*, modern agencies such as public service broadcasters were historically involved in the work of '...boundary and community construction at national...levels' (2007, p. 19). In the era of networked mediascapes, where the integrative role of national broadcasting is disturbed, boundary work becomes more difficult but also more pressing, arguably defining the media's role as a site for the '...endless playing with difference and sameness' (ibid).Boundary work among western European public service broadcasters is shaped, but not determined by, the politics of integration (Leurdijk 2006; Horsti 2009). Ben O'Loughlin (2006) has demonstrated how BBC policy shifted from an essentialist vision of multiculturalism to a 'concept of cultural diversity' influenced by community cohesion agendas, and the knowledge economy goal of increasing individual social capital (2006, p. 15). O'Loughlin's British coordinates map broadly onto the frameworks developed within Radio Telifís Éireann (RTÉ). The broadcaster's policy framework was also inflected with a desire to 'get it right' beyond multiculturalism, as evidenced by the careful, multi-stage development of a 'diversity and interculturalism' policy between 2005 and 2009 (Titley, Kerr and King O'Riain 2010, p. 113–138). Interculturalism was adopted as a dimension of the institutions' corporate review, and spliced to the established remit in the Public Service Charter to enhance 'the democratic, social and cultural values of Irish society' and to reflect the 'regional, cultural and political diversity of Ireland and its peoples' (2004, p. 4). Thus in its *2007 Corporate Responsibility Report* it adopted the role of an intercultural mediator, with '...a decisive and responsible role in determining attitudes and levels of understanding between communities and cultures (2007, p. 52). While space prevents a fuller examination, a similar narrative trajectory to that of national governance can be discerned, if for different reasons. From a position that similarly imagines 'migrants' as '...always already excluded and in need of integration' (Gray 2006, p. 121), the policy proposes a role in educating majority and minority audiences in an appropriate valuing of other cultures, and thus providing resources for understanding and tolerance. However, the commitment to integration through diversity is a mediated commitment, operating at the level of representation, and with stated goals concerning diversified staff profiles scaled back over time (RTÉ 2007, p. 53). The interculturalism of better understanding and more tolerance as the keys to 'integration' are inflected with the domopolitical logic that locates 'acceptable' societal outcomes at the level of individual actualization, at the expense of critical spaces for articulating systemic problems and racialized experiences.

## Transnational 'media worlds': cultural governance and contrapuntal negotiations

The contrapuntal dynamics of transnational media engagement open up other kinds of critical spaces. The following discussion draws from twelve focus groups and concentrates on a discussion of the reflections of young Chinese women, and a diverse range of Nigerian female, and some male, participants. The comparative relation between nationally-based groups, as well as single and mixed gender groups, requires contextual explanation. The research worked with nationally-based groups to facilitate snowball sampling and linguistic access. The aim was not to attempt to produce 'national profiles' or generalizable results, but instead to conduct thematic analysis based on their shared, politicized identity as non-EU nationals, and differentiated by the varying statuses – and accompanying constraints – available to them. As King O'Riain has argued, public discourse in Ireland has tended to position Chinese workers as 'model minorities', a form of benevolent essentialism that produces an '...image of a quiet, polite, hard-working, but exploitable population...and pits them against other migrants in Ireland' (2011). In contrast, the prevalent association of Nigerians with asylum seeking, and the particular iterations of anti-asylum seeker discourse in Ireland, work to produce Nigerians as a problematic population subject to periodic expressions of popular racism (Lentin and McVeigh 2006).

The focus group discussions were conducted respectively in Mandarin and English, and worked from open discussions of participants' media habits and what the researchers termed, perhaps fancifully, their 'media worlds'. This term is less grand ontological claim than methodological priority: rather than set a range of structuring topics, our aim was to facilitate discussants in outlining the contours of their own transnational media experiences, and to discuss the interplay of national, local, 'community' and transnational/diasporic engagements proceeding from this more emic set of concerns. The snowball sampling employed accounts for the fact that several of the Chinese focus groups were female only, whereas the Nigerian groups were consistently more gender-balanced. As a result, the following discussion proceeds through a thematic comparison shaped by this investigation of integration dynamics, and while the focus is on the experience of migrant women under domopolitical arrangements, the Nigerian-focused discussion does not artificially exclude perspectives offered by male participants that have a dialogic relevance.

*The country is small, there is no news*

From a small, diverse population of long-term Chinese residents, the population has increased rapidly over the past fifteen years, facilitated by changes in Chinese state emigration law, the labour market in Ireland, and the attraction of English language immersion (Yun Wang 2007). The majority of recent arrivals are young people on student visas – which allow for part-time work – and are overwhelmingly concentrated in the Dublin area. The research participants correspond broadly to this profile. Predominantly from Shenyang, Shanghai and Beijing, they ranged in age from twenty-three to forty-six, were mainly single, but some were married with partners here and at home. Some participants had been here less than a year and some as much as seven years, and had migrated to study English and work, with a view to expanding their experience, earning to support family in China, and/or to invest in an enterprise. Most were working as healthcare assistants, cleaners, waiting staff, language teachers, nurses, and many were studying as students in training institutions. Six focus groups were conducted with 5–8 participants. Four of these involved all-female participation, and are the subject of this analysis.

In a study of 'young diasporic Chinese' in Iowa, Yu Shi emphasizes 'their complex cultural condition of living on "borderlands" and ... their ongoing process of identity negotiation' (2005, p. 60). In a difference that is as positional as it is biographical, Dublin does not constitute a borderland marked by tensions between competing futures. Instead, it is a migratory site affectively bounded by the certainties of return, even if in practice such plans may be flexible (Yun Wang and King O'Riain 2006). As Lu recalled, 'When I just came I knew little about Ireland ... there was a nickname for Ireland, which was "the second re-employment base for the people from North-East China"'. Consequently, much discussion of engagement with Irish-based media is recounted as part of a process of ongoing orientation: language acquisition, and surveillance of political-economic threats to their status are recurring topics: 'I don't really (follow) unless (Irish news) is related to immigration, visas, education policies.' Similarly, general media use, and specific engagement with Irish media, is shaped by the rhythms and exigencies of lives lived working in the flexibilized service and care industries. In the working spaces of shops, cafés and public buildings, national radio and Irish and UK television channels – particularly Sky News – are ubiquitous environmental presences. Several focus group discussions refer to the desire to watch 'anything' on television after work, preferably involving shared viewing as a scarce communal pleasure, with Chinese and non-Chinese housemates. As Xue elaborates:

> I watch TV with my friends together because the TV is placed in the sitting room. We agree on a channel first. It feels good when we sit and watch TV together. We laugh together if something is laughable. We can share something.

Similar exigencies structure transnational media engagement. The 'Chinese transnational mediasphere' is extensive, but must be understood in terms of localized conditions and inflections (Wanning 2005). Living in rented accommodation restricts satellite use, thus discussants had irregular access to transnational television, other than streaming online. Chinese 'community media' – including newspapers such as *The Shining Emerald* – were of interest if available in a café, like other 'free sheets', but not as objects of affective or cultural attachment.

Media produced by and for the Chinese in Ireland were mainly evaluated in terms of detached utility, and given that it was held that the information they contain is available faster online, they simply did not feature as significant points of reference: 'They don't have much information from back home. Ireland Chinese news hardly has any'.

If media use was frequently defined by pragmatic constraints, media engagement was shaped by priorities derived from the wider, gendered experience of work and opportunity-based migration. According to Kim (2010), the transnational mobility of young Chinese women has been shaped by exclusion, where despite increased female access to tertiary education in China, '... gendered socio-economic and cultural conditions persist and continue to structure labour market outcomes and lifestyles' (2010, p. 28). Yet, transnational mobility enables a 'different life trajectory' and mediated resources allow for the construction of transnational subjectivities through '... an extension of social imagery from which women can reconstruct their conceptions of self in relation to the lived realities of global Others' (2010, p. 39). For many discussants it is not society in Ireland or self in society in Ireland that stands as the contrapuntal other for re-imagining the self. Instead it is a site from where their relations to China are re-assessed. To this end, the contrapuntal involves navigating a projected future of self-insertion in the labour market and society: of, as Xia noted, 'not being backward when I go back to China'.

Keeping up with the news about China involves relational interpretation across a variety of national and transnational channels, and keeping up has a dual sense – of staying informed in the present, and staying engaged for the future. 'The country is small, there is no news' – for Xia the disparity in societal scale maps onto thresholds of what *constitutes* news, and Ireland simply does not pass a threshold of significance adequate to the role of contrapuntal 'global Other'. For many participants, beyond the strategic surveillance of Irish broadcast news, their discussions focus on how Irish and British channels represent China's role on the world stage. While this focus is prevalent, it is not monological. Evaluations of coverage of Chinese issues may involve long-distance nationalism, as Lie puts it, 'It's funny for such a small country to criticize other countries'. However, it is also a resource for reflecting on official Chinese narratives:

> I began to know China when I came abroad. When I was in China, I didn't know anything. I lived in a specific cycle (of society). I thought that ... there was only prosperity. Everything was good on the surface. When I came out, I realized that China had a lot of negative aspects which I hadn't known.

Given this attention to the demands of future re-integration, official narratives of migrant governance simply do not feature, and when they do, as Xue reflects, it is linked to indicators derived from their own prerogatives of mobility and achievement:

> More and more Chinese people have come here. They have integrated into Irish society. Irish people have known Chinese culture, food and New Year. Besides, Chinese people used to do low-paid jobs. The jobs have changed somehow. Some people work at bank now. The change has influenced on Irish multiculturalism.

Throughout, the constraints of work/study and status, questions of cultural scale, and a dominant sense of an experience bounded in time if not duration produce ideas of 'integration' *adequate* to these conditions. Yet reflections on media use and everyday life also nuance the pronounced insistence on the mobile self. Mei's experience of internal mobility is unusual among the discussants, and suggests how media use may be central to place-making over time:

> My husband and I used to live in a village (in Ireland). There was a website of that village. I don't browse it now. My husband browses it often. He is concerned about if there is any change of that village. He is concerned about it and wants to keep informed about it. We were there for two years after all. He is concerned about it very much. I learn (about that village) from him. He browses (the website) first and tells me the change of that village.

This accumulation of local attachment is erased in the domopolitical imagination, which in fixating on the national home allows no space for the kind of situated, affective belonging attested to in this reflection.

*Today they want us to stay and tomorrow they are sending us away*

According to the Census, 16,300 Nigerians were living in Ireland in 2006, though that is widely regarded to be a conservative figure. A relative increase of eighty-two per cent since the 2002 figure of 8,969, Nigeria has been the destination from whence most applications from asylum have been received by the Irish state year-on-year since 2001. Education, work and family networks are other significant migration pathways. The male/female ratio of the population is 55:45 and the average age is 26.6 years. Most live in Dublin and east coast towns. Comparative with the other Census profiles, a relatively high number were unemployed or looking for their first job (31 per cent). One in five women work in the home and 17 per cent are students. The dominant industry is health and social work, and among the top occupations were care assistants and attendants (11 per cent), security guards (7 per cent), sales assistants (7 per cent) and doctors (6 per cent) (CSO 2008, pp. 23–43).

Six focus groups were held in Dublin and the east coast, and two of these were held in state-run accommodation centres. The participants ranged in age from twenty-six to forty-five with the vast majority in their mid-thirties, and all of the focus groups were gender-mixed. More than half of the participants were studying and/or working, three women were working in the home, and the participants involved in asylum-determination cases are prohibited from work or study. Nearly all the participants had been living in Ireland for at least four years, and a third of them for more than seven years (this calculation excludes those seeking asylum).

These discussions present a picture of media worlds networked across Ireland, Nigeria, the UK and elsewhere. Individual practices within this mediascape are intimately shaped by personal experiences of dwelling in and between nations, regions and localities, and of feelings about this experience at particular moments in time and in varying familial, domestic and social contexts. Media use invariably plays many roles in the participants' lives, yet there is an important focus on how media practices act as a locus of wider questions of orientation and belonging. In common with the Chinese experiences, there is a high level of media monitoring and evaluating news, however, it is informed by the near-history of overt racism directed at Nigerians in Ireland (Lentin 2007). As John elaborates: 'In Ireland I've made a conscious decision not to read particular newspapers...just because of their racist disposition towards the immigrant community, especially the African community'. Mike captures a widespread sentiment when he discusses how different types of news have political resonances in lives intimately affected by state decisions and public opinion:

> I watch either the 6 o clock news or the 9 o clock on RTE. It tells me what is happening in Ireland. This is my place today. It's where I live. Maybe it's where my children will live, I don't know. They were born here and this is their country. But I like to hear about everything that is happening...what the government is saying, especially about immigrants. You know that they are always changing their minds about us. Today they want us to stay and tomorrow they are sending us away.

Mike's reflection is marked by the disjunctures of civic stratification. The legitimacy granted to parents of 'Irish-born' – as distinguished from 'Irish' – children has been a central trope of migration debates since the 2004 Citizenship referendum (Lentin 2007). His ongoing monitoring is shared by discussants in direct provision; Mary, living in state-run accommodation, provides a heuristic analysis:

> I think I know what my sister here was saying about Irish TV and their coverage of immigrants. I watch news on RTE and on TV3 but I think RTE presents more information when they report about immigrants. TV3 only show the surface and they appear not to be interested in issues involving immigrants. If you watch the same news item on both channels, you will be surprised at how little the information presented by TV3 is. You really get the impression that they have no time for immigrants. RTE is better and fairer. I'm against TV3 because they don't explain any thing. They just show a small clip and rush through as if they never wanted to do it anyway.

Rendered beyond the scope of 'integration' and public participation, many of the discussants in direct state provision are nevertheless immersed in the proceedings of the national public sphere, and this sphere is reformed through contrapuntal relations. There is an irony that the frayed, modern integrative modalities of national broadcasting remain relevant in this kind of space; one focus group discussed how the 6.01 evening news acted as a shared way of organizing time in their accommodation centre. Others in the same context talk at length about Irish national and local, UK, Nigerian and African news; the category of 'international' news is positional; it is a genre of personal, translocal importance, and its significance shifts across scales. It is discussed as an indicator of the 'openness' of Irish society to the world out there, and in here – coverage of Africa is significant for coverage of African migrants, and vice versa:

> RTE does not show enough news about immigrants or about Africa. In fact it doesn't show much about other parts of world. I watch Al Jazeera when I want news about the world. I also watch the South African station – channel 230 on Sky – for news about Africa. Sometimes I watch CNN and BBC but only sometimes.

This near ubiquitous criticism of narrowness is also made concerning some Nigerian broadcasters, and often contrasted with CNN and Al Jazeera. It is an implicit criticism of how international news is produced by national broadcasters, and its comparative adequacy for media audiences that live in environments of instantaneous, transnational coverage. Yet this transnational media space is also a space of unsettled relations; of being excluded from social imaginaries in Ireland, and for many, also finding their relationships with Nigerian media to be complicated by personal processes of settlement, social integration, and negotiation of diasporic relations. Bey, a man in his thirties working in the Dublin area, describes his position explicitly in terms of boundary work:

> There is a home and there is a residence. There is a difference between the two. Ireland is my residence. My brother here...said Nigeria is his home. I don't know where my home is. I'm a Diasporan. I don't know where I belong. Nigeria is still not ready for anything. It's still killing its talents and forcing them to flee to other countries. Ireland does not want us. Read the newspapers, listen to radio or television. None of them speaks about us as members of this society. We're the permanent visitors. They create a distinction where they don't need to.

For many, the idea of future return is important, yet it functions as a dimension of home-making, particularly where family multiplies the vectors on which home is made. Emmy, in her thirties and working at home, expresses this in terms of everyday routine:

> I watch OBE or Ben TV because they give insights into events at home. Nigeria is my home. I'm also part of here but I'm more part of there. I've two children, born here. So I do feel that this is my place but I belong more to Nigeria. I watch RTE for local news and...the weather reports are important for me because, being a mother, I've laundry to do.

While those awaiting asylum determination frequently develop a media literacy at odds with their formal right to participate, many discussants with secure status connect their criticisms of poor representation with demands they are entitled to make. Irish media are constantly reminded that they are in competition for the discussants' engagement within a convergent mediascape. In contradistinction to the Chinese focus groups, RTÉ's intercultural programmes are referenced and dissected, and the general evaluation proposes a contrapuntal variation on multiculturalism's relations of recognition – why should we watch what we do not recognize ourselves in? The fact of paying a television licence fee is similarly used to contest the dynamics of tolerant recognition in terms of rights: we pay for better representation.

## Conclusion

This article has presented a reading of shifting lines of contrapuntal engagement. It provides a glimpse of migrant media practices informed and shaped by identifications with intersecting communities and social realities. By integrating Irish media relationally into transnational repertoires of reference and possibility, they suggest the situated ordinariness of multivalent and reflective practices of integration. In a political context where transnational attachments and affiliations can be rendered suspect, the rehearsal of contrapuntal interpretation disturbs the established either/or disciplinarity periodically applied to the wrong kinds of transnationalism. However, the context of Irish domopolitics unsettles any conclusion that would seek to frame these practices through claims to '...difference and heterogeneity as vehicles of critical transformation and progressive change' (Ang and St Louis 2005, p. 293). As the discussion of ephemeral, culturalized trajectories of governance in Ireland suggests, the subject of domopolitics is not necessarily or not only difference as identity, as the celebration of difference has been intrinsic to the theming of integration. Instead, as the tiered legitimacy of civic stratification attests, it is difference as the potential for political contestation and conflict over the distribution of socio-economic resources.

A prevalent, contrapuntal dimension of the interpretative media work discussed here is the disjuncture between cultural integration and the possibilities for citizenship and residency. This is at its most acute in the experiences of the discussants living through their asylum determination processes. The time and space that allows them to cultivate an intimate engagement with mediated public culture in Ireland are products of political structures that exclude them from the public. As well as the implications of this interplay of discursive inclusion and structural exclusion for meaningful ideas of the integrated society, for media and audience research it suggests that attention to culture as a site of agency must be more carefully related to the uses of culture in a neoliberal era.

### Note

1. The November 2008 budget ended funding for the National Consultative Committee on Racism, and coincided with a decision not to extend the work of the National Action Plan Against Racism. The annual budget of the OMI was cut by twenty-six per cent of an overall budget of approx eight million Euros. The provision of English language teachers in schools with migrant children was significantly scaled back. See Watt, Philip 2008 'Budget cutbacks weaken State's capacity to combat racism', *The Irish Times*, 11 November. Whatever the relative merits of these agencies, their disposability supports a reading of integration as a strategic political narrative.

### References

ANG, Ien and ST LOUIS, BRETT 2005 'The predicament of difference', *Ethnicities*, vol. 5, no. 3, pp. 291–304

BOUCHER, GERRY 2008 'Ireland's lack of a coherent integration policy', *Translocations*, vol. 3, no. 1, pp. 5–28
CENTRAL STATISTICS OFFICE (CSO) 2008 Census 2006: 'Population and Migration Estimates', Cork: CSO Publications
CONNOLLY, WILLIAM 1995 *The Ethos of pluralization*, Minneapolis: University of Minnesota Press
CROWLEY, NIALL 2010 *Hidden Messages, Overt Agendas*, Dublin: Migrant Rights Centre Ireland
Department of Communications, Marine and Natural Resources 2004 *Public Service Broadcasting Charter*, Dublin
FANNING, BRYAN 2009 *New Guests of the Irish Nation*, Dublin: Irish Academic Press
FEKETE, LIZ 2009 *A Suitable Enemy: Racism, Migration and Islamophobia in Europe*, London: Pluto
FLERAS, AUGIE 2009 *The Politics of Multiculturalism. Multicultural Governance in Comparative Perspective*, Basingstoke, UK: Palgrave Macmillan
GRAY, BREDA 2006 'Migrant integration policy: a nationalist fantasy of management and control?', *Translocations*, vol. 1, no. 1, pp. 118–38
GUILD, ELSPETH, KEES, GROENENDIJK and CARRERA, SERGIO 2009 'Understanding the contest of community: illiberal practices in the EU? in Elspeth Guild, Groenendijk Kees and Sergio Carrera (eds), *Illiberal Liberal States*, Farnham: Ashgate, pp. 1–25
HAGE, GHASSAN 2000 *White Nation: Fantasies of White Supremacy in a Multicultural Society*, London: Pluto
HORSTI, KARINA 2009 'Antiracist and multicultural discourses in European public service broadcasting: celebrating consumable differences in the Prix Iris Media prize', *Communication, Culture & Critique*, vol. 2, no. 3, pp. 339–60
KIM, YOUNA 2010 'Female individualization? Transnational mobility and media consumption of Asian women', *Media, CultureSociety*, vol. 32, no. 1, pp. 25–43
KOFMAN, ELEONORE 2005 'Citizenship, migration and the reassertion of national identity', *Citizenship Studies*, vol. 9, no. 5, pp. 453–67
LARSEN, HÅKON 2010 'Legitimation strategies of public service broadcasters: the divergent rhetoric in Norway and Sweden', *Media, Culture and Society*, vol. 32, no. 2, pp. 267–83
LENTIN, ALANA and TITLEY, GAVAN 2011 *The Crises of Multiculturalism? Racism in a Neoliberal Age*, London: Zed Books
LENTIN, RONIT 2007 'Ireland: racial state and crisis racism', *Ethnic and Racial Studies*, vol. 30, no. 4, pp. 610–27
LENTIN, RONIT and ROBBIE, M 2006 *After Optimism: Ireland, Racism and Globalisation*, Dublin: Metro Éireann Publications
LEURDIJK, ANDRA 2006 'In search of common ground: strategies of multicultural television producers in Europe', *European Journal of Cultural Studies*, vol. 9, no. 1, pp. 25–46
MAGUIRE, MARK and MURPHY, FIONA 2009 'Management, truth and life', *Irish Journal of Anthropology*, vol. 12, no. 2, pp. 6–10
MCGHEE, DEREK 2008 *The End of Multiculturalism? Terrorism, Integration and Human Rights*, Maidenhead, Berkshire: Open University Press
O'LAUGHLIN, BEN 2006 'The operationalization of the concept "cultural diversity" in British television policy and governance', Working Paper no. 27, CRESC Working Paper Series, November 2006
OFFICE OF THE MINISTER FOR INTEGRATION (OMI) 2006 Dublin: Government of Ireland Publications
PILLINGER, JANE 2007 *The Feminisation of Migration: Experiences and Opportunities in Ireland*, Dublin: Immigrant Council of Ireland
RTÉ 2007 Corporate Responsibility Report, Dublin: RTÉ
SALMON, CHRISTIAN 2009 *Storytelling: Bewitching the Modern Mind*, London: Verso

SHI, YU 2005 'Identity construction of the Chinese diaspora, ethnic media use, community formation, and the possibility of social activism', *Continuum: Journal of Media & Cultural Studies*, vol. 19, no. 1, pp. 55–72

SILVERSTONE, ROGER 2007 *Media and Morality: on the Rise of the Mediapolis*, Cambridge: Polity

TITLEY, GAVAN, KERR, APHRA and KING O'RIAIN, REBECCA 2010 *Broadcasting in the New Ireland: Mapping and Envisioning Cultural Diversity*, Dublin: National University of Ireland, Maynooth/Broadcasting Commission of Ireland

TSOUKALA, ANASTASSIA 2005 'Looking at migrants as enemies', in Didier Bigo and Elspeth Guild (eds), *Controlling Frontiers: Free Movement into and within Europe*, Farnham: Ashgate, pp. 161–92

VERTOVEC, STEVEN and WESSENDORF, SUSANNE 2009 'Assessing the backlash against multiculturalism in Europe', MMG Working Paper 09–04

WALTERS, WILLIAM 2004 'Secure borders, safe haven, domopolitics', *Citizenship Studies*, vol. 8, no. 3, pp. 237–60

WANNING, SUN 2005 'Media and the Chinese diaspora: community, consumption, and transnational imagination', *Journal of Chinese Overseas*, vol. 1, no. 1, pp. 65–86

YUN WANG, YING 2007 'Chinese earthquake appeal network in Ireland' unpublished paper, Trinity Immigration Initiative, Trinity College Dublin

YUN WANG, YING and KING-O'RIAIN, REBECCA 2006 *Chinese Students in Ireland*, Dublin: NCCRI

YÚDICE, GEORGE 2003 *The Expediency of Culture: Uses of Culture in the Global Era*, Durham: Duke University Press

# Do Turkish women in the diaspora build social capital? Evidence from the Low countries

Christine Ogan and Leen d'Haenens

**Abstract**
Ever since Putnam (2000) made social capital a concept that should be mourned for its decline in the USA, researchers and policy makers in some western countries have adopted it as a solution to what they believe to be the failed practices of multiculturalism. Instead of preserving their individual cultures and traditions, critics would have them build social capital by bridging to people and institutions in their new countries and adopt the 'shared values' of the host countries and become 'integrated'. This study, based on a study conducted in the Netherlands in 2006, and supplemented with survey findings from Flanders at the same time, examines whether this perspective is accurate, focusing on women migrants who live in the Low Countries (Netherlands and Flanders in Belgium), of the networks they have built or not and the reasons for that, and of the role of media and the internet in that process.

Robert Putnam is likely the best known researcher of the concept of social capital, as detailed in his book, *Bowling Alone* (2000). In his view, 'social capital refers to connections among individuals – social networks and the norms of reciprocity and trustworthiness that arise from them' (Putnam 2000, p. 19). Arneil (2006) contrasts his definition with that of Bourdieu (1986) and Gramsci (1971) who represent the European school. As Arneil articulates the difference, Bourdieu does not see social capital as a group of individuals who make decisions to connect with one another, but rather as a concept focused on the economic, cultural and social forces that 'limit the range of possibilities that certain individuals or groups have for creating networks or drawing on the resources inherent in them' (Arneil 2006, p. 201). Where Putnam might look at the number of connections between individuals to show the building of social capital, Bourdieu would analyse the nature of those connections in historic context (Arneil 2006). In this study, we also examine the nature of the connections and the power inequities between Turkish women minorities and the majority populations in Flanders and the Netherlands.

This study of Turkish women migrants in Flanders and the Netherlands and their struggles to build social capital in their new homes is framed in the critique of that concept from Bourdieu's perspective and articulated by scholars who have recently interrogated Putnam's analysis and the new European policies about inculcating a sense of 'shared norms' in the ethnic minority populations in their midst.

Because this article addresses two marginalized groups – ethnic minorities who are also women – and the policies governing their lives, the difficulties they face in trying to build social capital fit more appropriately with Bourdieu's understanding of the concept than that of Putnam. The participants in this study are Turkish migrants who have lived in the Netherlands or Flanders an average of seven years. We chose to include the Flemish part of Belgium as a comparison because of the linguistic and cultural similarity to the Netherlands.

Putnam's conception of bridging and bonding is flawed, according to Arneil (2006), but she believes it is a good way to examine community relationships. Putnam defines bonding social capital as 'inward looking and tend(ing) to reinforce exclusive identities and homogeneous groups', while bridging 'networks are outward looking and encompass people across diverse social cleavages' (Putnam 2000, p. 22). The distinction is important to this study as ethnic minorities are seen to bond more to each other in a culture than to bridge to the larger society where they live. Our study supports Arneil's (2006) view of bridging as a mechanism by which those people who want to move between different communities in their society can actually do so rather than to fuse the diverse communities into one.

Whether or not the Turkish women in this study are able to build social capital depends on many factors. Possession of the physical and technological means and resources to do so constitutes one set of considerations. Also of importance is the social and religious environment in which the women live, as well as the government policies that either enable or inhibit the building of social capital. Following a discussion of these factors, we describe the methodology for the study and the results. The research questions guiding the inquiry are as follows:

1. Are more recent Turkish women migrants making use of Dutch mass media and Dutch language internet sites to build social capital through bridging? Are Turkish women migrants in Flanders acting similarly?
2. Are more recent Turkish women migrants in the Netherlands making use of Turkish mass media and Turkish language internet sites to build social capital through bonding? Are Turkish women in Flanders acting similarly?
3. What impact do religious attitudes have on the bridging and bonding of social capital among newer Turkish women migrants in the Netherlands and in Flanders?

**Technology and mass media's role in the production of social capital**

In *Bowling Alone* Putnam (2000)[1] cites the inverse relationship between the rise of television viewing and the decline of civic engagement. He considers the entertainment media a major factor in the decline of social trust, voting turnout and membership in groups. Several recent studies have refuted Putnam's assertions about the relationship between the components of social capital. Kim (2007) analysed data from a telephone survey in South Korea, finding that interpersonal trust and informal socializing were positively related to civic participation and to entertainment use of the internet. Ellison, Steinfield and Lampe (2007) studied the use of Facebook for its building of social capital, finding that Facebook members were able to build social capital through both bridging and bonding and also to stay connected with members of a previously inhabited community on the social network site. Based on online interviews of residents of New Orleans who had been dispersed by Hurricane Katrina, Procopio and Procopio (2007) found that respondents both maintained social capital by keeping connections with family and friends online and built new social capital by activating weak ties in their social networks. Women in their study benefited more from the online communication than did men.

Two studies of migrant populations have also found social capital value in internet use. d'Haenens, Koeman and Saeys (2007) surveyed Moroccan and Turkish youth in Flanders and the Netherlands about information and communications technology (ICT) adoption and use, finding largely bonding activity to relatives and friends in their families' countries of origin through email, but also bridging activity to the youth in the majority population. A similar study of educated immigrants in the USA by Chen and Thorson (2007) found that members of the Chinese ethnic community were involved in both bonding to other members of their ethnic community and bridging to groups in the wider society. Use of ethnic media for news and entertainment were not significant predictors of civic participation or political knowledge.

More broadly speaking, key findings from European research on ethnic minorities as media users show time and again that television continues to be the most important medium for migrant groups, with Turkish immigrants being the television 'champions' (Bonfadelli, Bucher and Piga 2007). Television viewing tends to be predominantly entertainment oriented and a socializing, communal activity for ethnic minority groups rather than an individualistic one. Access to electronic media is high in homes of minority families, while ICT access remains significantly lower, despite a shrinking digital gap. Although first-generation minority groups prefer media in their own languages and from their countries of origin, there is a demand for news covering the minority groups' everyday concerns on mainstream channels. Ethnic minorities, especially Turks, predominantly use minority media, especially television programmes, from their countries of origin (e.g. Ogan 2001). Nevertheless, most studies show that homeland and host country media are used complementarily (Peeters and d'Haenens 2005). The 'ghetto-thesis', stating that minority groups expose themselves only to minority media from their countries of origin, is an overly simplified perspective (e.g. Güntürk 1999; Hafez 2002). Among ethnic minorities, higher levels of majority media use are predicted by higher socioeconomic status, longer time spent in the host country and better language skills (e.g. Weiss and Trebbe 2001). The 'direct integration thesis', suggesting that a greater use of majority media by ethnic minorities has a positive influence on their level of integration, is confirmed in many studies (for an overview, see Bonfadelli, Bucher and Piga 2007).

## Dutch and Flemish policies promoting/discouraging social capital

In the European policy context, social capital is used in the Coleman (1988, 1990) sense and defined as 'those stocks of social trust, norms and networks that people can draw upon to solve common problems' (European Commission 2007, p. 7). The Netherlands was found to be a social capital-rich country in terms of its level of social trust and associational membership indicators, according to a monitoring report by the European Commission (2007) on social cohesion, trust and participation. About 61 per cent of the Dutch respondents agreed with the statement 'most people can be trusted', while only about 29 per cent of Belgians[2] responded positively to that statement (European Commission 2007, p. 14). An even larger percentage of the social capital-rich nations reported membership in at least one voluntary organization (European Commission 2007).

While social policies in the Netherlands provide assistance for those unable to work, in need of housing and other financial help, minimal bridging occurs between the majority and the ethnic minorities. Schools tend to be relatively segregated and there is considerable geographic separation in urban housing. Multiculturalism policies have been defined as a 'drama' and are substituted by a more integrationist approach, emphasizing assimilation (Vasta 2007). In her critical article about Dutch policy shifts related to ethnic minorities, Vasta (2007, p. 717) cites the definition of integration as outlined in the 1994 Dutch policy to be 'a process leading to the full and equal participation of individuals and groups in society, for which mutual respect for identity is seen as a necessary condition' (Entzinger 2003, p. 72). (Strong) multiculturalism is seen as a 'set of integration policies that sees it as the active duty of the state to promote and protect minority cultures and sanctifies individuals' undeniable rights to have social institutions accommodate their special requirements' (Koopmans 2006, p. 23, cited by Vasta 2007, p. 732). Vasta describes assimilationist policy as one where the state coerces immigrants to adopt certain behaviours and sanctions non-compliance. We apply Vasta's definition of these terms in our reference to policies directed toward ethnic minorities in Flanders and the Netherlands.

The increasingly critical Dutch perspective is reflected in the 2003 Eurobarometer: 67.5 per cent of the respondents favoured limits to a multicultural society and Belgium was about half a percentage point above the Dutch (Coenders, Lubbers and Scheepers 2003, p. 3). Comparison with a set of similar questions in Eurobarometer surveys conducted in 1997 and 2000 revealed that the Dutch resistance had grown, while the Belgian resistance had declined from 1997 levels (Coenders, Lubbers and Scheepers 2003).

Recently, the Dutch have become more concerned about a lack of shared values with the majority population in ethnic communities. The ritual murders of Pim Fortuyn, a flamboyant right-wing populist politician and scholar with anti-immigrant views, and Theo van Gogh, a controversial film producer who worked with Ayaan Hirsi Ali, a former member of parliament for the Liberal Party (VVD), on a film critical of Islam's treatment of women (*Submission*), stirred up increased mutual resentment between the Dutch majority and the Muslim minority. In this climate of mistrust, the government enacted tougher immigration laws and new requirements for immigrants already living in the country. Immigrants under the age of fifty are now required to attend Dutch language classes and to pay for them; welfare payments may be cut for non-compliance. Previously, high dropout rates in language classes hindered their effectiveness. The Civic Integration Abroad Act, promulgated on 15 March 2006, sets an additional condition for obtaining a regular temporary residence permit–people must have a basic knowledge of the Dutch language and society prior to arrival in the Netherlands. The Basic Integration Examination on Dutch values (i.e. knowledge of 'Dutchness') and knowledge of the Dutch language is administered in the country of residence. Although our research in the Netherlands was conducted when the policy was just taking effect, respondents in the survey had begun to feel the effects and were reacting negatively to the anticipated changes.

When Flemish attitudes towards immigrants were examined by Billiet (2006) in an over-time analysis of comparable survey data, the responses showed a somewhat stronger anti-immigrant pattern to that of the Dutch. In Flanders,[3] where the issue of multiculturalism gradually came to be seen as independent from the issues of immigration and mobility – a shift that happened during the 1970s and 1980s – the debate has not yet been tackled in such a forthright fashion. The extreme right-wing stances taken by the racist political party *Vlaams Belang* have aroused more criticism of multiculturalism. Unlike the Netherlands, Belgium has adopted contradictory policies that sometimes take a crude assimilationist position and other times support ethnic diversity (Bousetta and Jacobs 2006).

**Methodology**

Interviews with Turkish migrants in Amsterdam and surrounding geographic areas were conducted between April and July 2006. Respondents were sought who had more recently arrived in the Netherlands (mean length of time = seven years). Since a random sample could not be drawn, respondents were recruited from places where migrants tend to be found – mosques, Dutch language schools and programmes, neighbourhood community centres, meetings of Turkish organizations and on the street in predominantly Turkish neighbourhoods. Respondents found in such locations may not be entirely representative as potential respondents who are less socially active will not be included, and those sorts of people may be less able to build social capital. Some other respondents were recruited through snowball sampling, thus adding individuals to the study who might not be socially engaged. However, at a time of increased tension among Turkish migrants, particularly in the aftermath of the new Dutch policies, cold-call recruiting was difficult. A total of fifty-three respondents answered 185 fixed-response questions and follow-up open-ended questions about their life circumstances; here, focus is made on the responses of the thirty-four women. The fixed-response questions included measures of their attitudes and behaviours related to the Dutch and Turkish people, media and internet use in Dutch and Turkish, and religious attitudes.

In Flanders at about the same time (February and May 2006), 341 Turkish respondents completed a survey including many of the same fixed-response questions. Respondents were drawn from Ghent, Antwerp and Genk, situated in the provinces with the largest Turkish populations, alongside those residing in the capital of Brussels. Respondents could choose to complete the survey in Flemish or in Turkish. In the comparative analysis that follows, results relating to social capital and focusing on the 178 women who completed the questionnaire are reported. The quotes collected in Flanders were derived from qualitative research conducted in Turkish and Moroccan families (d'Haenens, El Sghiar and Golaszewksi 2010).

Although bridging and bonding are difficult concepts to measure, we used several questions related to respondent connections with fellow Turks and members of the majority, as well as questions about attitudes toward the majority and feelings of belonging in the Netherlands or Belgium. These questions were supplemented with open-ended questions related to respondent interaction with Dutch or Flemish natives.

## Results

### Demographics: the Netherlands

The respondents in the Dutch study ranged in age from seventeen to forty-six. The educational attainment of respondents was relatively low: one in three had education not beyond five years of primary school. Another 24 or 45.3% per cent had completed middle school or high school or vocational school. Some respondents had completed university, obtained graduate degrees or had attended without graduating – 12 or 22.6% There were no significant gender differences associated with education.

### Media use

In order to bridge to the Dutch majority population, knowledge of Dutch is essential. Many of the respondents reported current registration in Dutch-language classes (24 or 45.3%). Regarding Dutch media consumption, there was more variation: 41.5 per cent reported no viewing of Dutch public channels at all or only very little. Private Dutch channel viewing was even less popular with 49.1 per cent not watching at all or very little. No statistically significant gender differences were identified. Those watching Dutch television reported doing so to improve their Dutch language skills (57.7 per cent). One of our informants said that although she had three diplomas on her wall (from Dutch classes), they were of no use to her because she lacked practical experience. Another respondent said she lacked the confidence to use the Dutch she had learned in class. She said she understood what was said in Dutch but could not respond. Lacking any Dutch or Turkish friends who could help, the media proved to be just another obstacle for her rather than a bridge to the majority culture. But others who learned the language early on believed that their perspective of the Dutch had changed. One woman talked of how fearful she was of Dutch people, believing they hated Muslims; but once she had mastered Dutch, she lost her fear and better understood the attitudes and beliefs of the Dutch she encountered in everyday life.

About half of the respondents reported newspaper and magazine reading for improving language skills (very) frequently (50.9 per cent). However, they also reported higher frequency of reading Turkish papers (52.8 per cent) than Dutch ones (41.5 per cent). Online dailies in Dutch were read (very) frequently by 13.5 per cent, and online dailies in Turkish were read (very) frequently by 36.6 per cent of respondents. Free sheets and ad sheets containing limited news were more widely read than other Dutch news media, with 52.8 per cent reporting reading them (very) frequently. Only 13.2 per cent said they never read these papers. There was a similar reading pattern of these papers by men and women.

As to computer use, nine of the women reported no computer use. (Very) frequently using the computer for searching in Dutch was reported by 52.6 per cent of the men but only 32.4 per cent of the women, although more searching was reported in Turkish (68.4 per cent of the men and 32.4 per cent of the women). We believe this is a good measure for bridging social capital as it possibly means that respondents are looking for information located in Dutch-based organizations, businesses, and so on, although reading about Dutch society on- or offline could also be done in Turkish.

*Attitudes related to social capital*

Bridging and bonding questions were asked concerning the respondents' view of their relationships with fellow Turks as well as the Dutch majority population (Table 1). The general pattern of responses was in the direction of more bonding. More than half of the respondents (completely/sometimes) agreed with the statements indicating bonding attitudes.

Bridging attitudes were expressed in the percentage of people who (completely) agreed with statements about the importance of having Dutch friends, seeing the Dutch point of view and identifying with both Dutch and Turkish communities (Table 2).

Women differed significantly from men in that many more felt they were on the side of the Dutch and more believed that the Dutch generally think positively about the Turks. However, more women said

**Table 1.** *Measures of bonding: percentages of those who agree or fully agree with the statements (Dutch N = 53, Flemish N = 341, Dutch women n = 34, Flemish women n = 178)*

| Statements | Men F | Men D | Women F | Women D | Total F | Total D |
|---|---|---|---|---|---|---|
| It is important to have status within one's own community NS | 94.3 | NA | 92.1 | NA | 93.5 | NA |
| In Belgium men and women are too open in their interactions** | 58.7 | 73.3 | 58.8 | 64.7 | 58.8 | 67.4 |
| It is important for Turks to have close ties | 80.6 | 66.7 | 72 | 55.9 | 76.3 | 59.6 |
| It is important to have Turkish friends | 84.2 | 88.9 | 79.9 | 79.4 | 82.1* | 82.7 |
| When people ask where I'm from, I say I'm Turkish | 89.8 | 83.4 | 92.2 | 97.0 | 91.1 | 92.3 |
| I am more comfortable when surrounded by Turks | 55.6 | 44.4 | 59.3 | 57.9 | 57.1 | 52.9 |
| When facing problems I can only turn to other Turks | 41.8 | 11.2 | 33.8 | 45.5 | 37.8 | 33.4* |
| I feel denigrated when told I am just like the Belgians/Dutch** | 13.8 | 11.1 | 15.6 | 18.7 | 14.8 | 16.0 |
| I feel discriminated against at school/at work** | 16.4 | 22.3 | 15.7 | 4.3 | 16.1* | 12.2 |
| It is a good thing that associations for the Turkish community exist | 78.6 | 66.7 | 72.6 | 80.7 | 75.5 | 75.5 |
| Youth should marry within the same faith | 53.1 | 42.1 | 56.3 | 58.9 | 54.8 | 52.8 |

*Indicates a likelihood of difference as a statistical relationship measured by $\chi^2$ was significant.
**Although this is not a real bonding measure, if a respondent was a recipient of discriminatory behaviour or observed behaviour inconsistent with cultural norms, then they may pull back to be with their ethnic community or increase bonding activity.

that whenever they have a problem, they only discuss it with other Turks. Also, more men than women believe it is important to have Dutch friends. These gender differences may exist because more men are in the workforce and therefore have daily contact with the Dutch, while women, particularly those who are homemakers, see other Turkish people most of the time. The gender differences indicate that little bridging may exist for women.

Religious attitudes were similar for men and women. Most of the respondents were Sunni Muslims (83.3 per cent), but 7.5 per cent said they subscribed to no religion, another 7.5 per cent said they were Alevis[4] and one respondent said he was Christian.

We asked about the relative importance of various Islamic practices: praying five times a day, going on the *haj*/pilgrimage, wearing the headscarf, fasting during Ramazan,[5] giving alms to the poor, and so on. In general, all practices were deemed important, even for those who were not particularly religious and for women who did not wear the

**Table 2.** *Measures of bridging among Belgian and Dutch Turks: percentages of those who agree or fully agree with the statements (Dutch N = 53, Flemish N = 341, Dutch women n = 34, Flemish women n = 178)*

| Statements | Men B | Men D | Women B | Women D | Total B | Total D |
|---|---|---|---|---|---|---|
| It is important to have Belgian/Dutch friends | 64.2 | 88.9 | 57.8 | 58.6 | 61.1 | 69.2* |
| When people ask me where I'm from I say I'm Belgian/Dutch | 11.2 | 11.2 | 7.3 | 8.8 | 9.3 | 9.6 |
| When people ask me where I'm from I say I am both Turkish and Belgian/Dutch | 34.7 | 16.7 | 25.0 | 33.4 | 29.8 | 27.4 |
| Belgians/Dutch think positively about Turks | 18.3 | 0.0 | 12.7 | 33.3 | 15.6 | 20.8* |
| Turks think positively about Belgians/Dutch | 30.6 | 16.7 | 19.6 | 30.3 | 25.0 | 25.5 |
| I feel like I am accepted by Belgians/Dutch | 41.3 | 16.7 | 41.1 | 53.1 | 41.3 | 40.0* |
| Most of the time I feel Belgian/Dutch | 7.2 | 5.6 | 6.9 | 21.2 | 7.1 | 15.7 |

*Indicates a likelihood of difference as statistical relationship measured by $\chi^2$ was significant.

headscarf. However, the three practices with least support were wearing the headscarf (42.5 per cent of the men and 58.8 per cent of the women said it was (very) important), for Turkish youth to marry within their religion (58.9% of women and 42.1% of men) and to be tied to a religious sect or *tarikat* (17.7% of the women and 26.3% of men). It should be noted that religious sects are outlawed in Turkey. All of the other questions related to the importance of religious practices received strong support, with a low of 69.8 per cent saying it was (very) important to master all the teachings of Islam to a high of 90.6 per cent saying it was (very) important to have a relationship with God.

As the policies and attitudes toward immigrants and their families require greater adoption of Dutch values, the migrants have fewer ways to resist assimilation – or to strengthen bonding. Religious practice is one of those ways and the headscarf is the most visible one. So a respondent may be saying that she has not adopted the practice but that it is her right and that of other Muslim women to do so. This interpretation is supported by Arneil's view that building of social capital may be resisted by immigrants because of the pressures to assimilate.

## Comparison with Flemish Turks

### Demographics

The respondents ($N = 341$) ranged in age from twenty to fifty-seven. Slightly more women (52 per cent) than men (48 per cent) responded. Overall, this group was better educated than those in the Dutch study.

In terms of media use, here too, little or no viewing of Flemish public (56.7 per cent) and private channels (49.3 per cent) was reported. But 25.5 per cent of the men did say they often or always watch public channels compared to only 14.2 per cent of the women ($\chi^2 = 14.7$, df = 4, $p = .006$).[6]

Reading Flemish newspapers was reported (very) frequently by 38 per cent of both men and women for improving their Dutch language skills; however, the remaining 62 per cent said they never read a Flemish paper. The respondents reported higher reading of Turkish papers (35.8 per cent (very) frequently, 23.5 per cent from time to time). Online Flemish newspapers were read (very) frequently by a mere 2.1 per cent. Five per cent reported reading a Flemish newspaper online from time to time. Reading the Turkish press online was somewhat more popular as 16.4 per cent said they read these papers (very) frequently. The freely distributed newspapers were not widely read, with more than half (52 per cent) of men and women saying they never read these papers and only 21.8 per cent reading (very) frequently. Computer use was comparable among Turkish men (69 per cent) and women (63 per cent), much higher than the respondents in the Netherlands. However, in the area of search, 31.6 per cent of men and 27 per cent of women reported conducting online searches in Dutch (a measure of bridging), but somewhat higher percentages reported (very) frequently searching in Turkish (36.7 per cent of men and 25.5 per cent of women).

The Flemish sample was somewhat older and had spent more time in Flanders than the respondents in the Netherlands. The Flemish-Turks also were somewhat more educated than the Dutch-Turks. That might have led to greater media use, but not much difference was actually reported in viewing of public and private Dutch language channels. Because our samples may not have been representative, we compared our findings with those of the Netherlands Social and Cultural Planning Office (Huysmans and de Haan 2008) in its survey conducted in autumn 2004 and spring 2005 on about 4,000 ethnic minority respondents (of which 948 were of Turkish descent, age ranging from fifteen to sixty-four). The findings in that study support our results. The study showed that people of Turkish descent continue to watch significantly less mainstream Dutch television (public, commercial or local channels) than the Dutch majority. They also make less use of the home computer than members of the majority. These differences reflect the lower levels of minority-group computer ownership at home. After controlling for socioeconomic status (SES), ethnic minorities make considerably less use of the internet than the majority. Not surprisingly, this digital divide remains highest among the first generations (also after controlling for SES).

## Social capital

Significant gender differences were found in Flanders for several statements (Tables 1 and 2), but there was no pattern of significance. A subset ($n = 82$) of the Flemish group was pulled out – people who had lived in Belgium less than ten years – and showed no significant gender differences. When asked about the importance of Turkish friends and taking problems only to other Turks, more women agreed with those statements than men – just like in the Dutch group. The migrant men in the Netherlands seemed to feel particularly distanced from the Dutch in their interactions, as evidenced by their feelings that the Dutch do not accept or think positively about them.

In the statements on several Islamic religious practices, the respondents were like the Dutch in that there was generally a very high importance placed on these. The three least supported practices were the need for religious sects (8.7 per cent overall), to fasting during Ramazan (45.9 per cent of the men and significantly less (39.2 per cent) of the women) and the need for youth to marry within the faith (54.8 per cent overall). The only other significant gender difference was for celebrating religious holidays, with women placing higher importance (88.3 per cent) compared to 80.1 per cent of the men.

The women in this study are at a particular disadvantage in building social capital: in the Netherlands, 58.8 per cent listed their profession as homemaker (compared to 6.2 per cent in Flanders, but 66 per cent were unemployed). Of those women who married into families that had long been settled in Europe, many experienced pressure from their mothers-in-law to stay at home and take care of their husbands and have children before they studied Dutch or explored their new community. Although they started language classes upon arrival (as required), they had to drop out when they became pregnant. Harika[7] said:

> I was alone for one or two years; all alone at home while my husband went to work. I couldn't go outside my home. I was so afraid. When my husband came home, he'd take me out. When my child was born, I started to go out and at least do a little shopping. When you arrive here, you become half a person, you have to learn everything from scratch.

Another woman mentioned the impossibility of returning to classes with daycare costs being prohibitively high. Asise, a forty-two-year-old living in Genk, Belgium, who did not work outside the home, provided an example of her dependency on her husband to interact with Flemish acquaintances:

When I leave the house on my own, then I only go to other Turks, but if we [she and her husband] go together then we go to Flemings because when he is with me I can understand them. He translates for me then.

Those women who worked outside their home were in general better integrated into the majority community and spoke the language, had friends other than Turks, and so on. However, women and unemployed men with limited daily contact with the majority population did not hold stronger values that would relate to bonding (feel they could take problems only to Turks, etc.), so the assumption that working alongside Dutch or Flemish colleagues would help in bridging was not upheld and the strong gender differences described previously were not based on work contact in the case of the women. Women were often found gathering in groups – having meetings in a community centre or in a Turkish organization, forming friendships in language classes or at a Koran study session in a mosque. Although there were exceptions, these women were not isolated from other Turkish women and their behaviour offered clear examples of traditional bonding practices, keeping them on the margins of the majority society.

**Discussion**

The findings of this study do more to prompt further research than to provide definitive answers to our research questions. They are limited because of the small number of respondents in the Dutch research (where more qualitative data were collected), but also limited in the Flemish research because of the difficulty of drawing random samples. We have therefore provided more descriptive findings, but the qualitative research in the Netherlands and the corroboration by a national Dutch study allow us to be somewhat more confident about our conclusions. The research does begin to tell a story about social capital and the limits to building it, and to the use of media as a resource for these women in two countries. It supports Bourdieu's perspective on social capital as being constrained by power inequities. The women in this study had the least ability and opportunity to build social capital through bridging. Geographically separated from the majority population and lacking education and skills that limit economic advancement, they are unable to build the networks necessary for increasing social capital, as Bourdieu has asserted. When women's contact with the majority increased because of employment outside the home, their bridging behaviour increased, despite a lack of socialization with the majority population, thus supporting Arneil's view that assimilation of ethnic minorities is not necessary to build social capital through bridging.

If women do not bridge through their face-to-face contacts and are limited in their contacts through media sources, there is not much hope for the situation to change for them, regardless of the number of regulations created to increase their social capital. One set of questions asked the respondents in the Netherlands if the Turkish language programmes on television, the Turkish newspapers, the Turkish language websites and radio in Turkish were sufficient for them. Though there was little gender difference, most people saw print, radio and the internet in Turkish fulfilling their needs more than television, likely because they did not find sufficient content on television to assist them in building social capital. This creates an opening for Dutch language public television to create programmes with Turkish subtitles that would fulfil those needs in public affairs and entertainment. That might be a particularly good practice for the production of documentaries, as the Turkish women in the study tended to watch these more than news in Dutch. From examples provided at a conference in Hilversum (held yearly as the Diversity Show) on the use of public service television programming for diversity, it seems that these programmes are primarily aimed at youth. But such programmes fail to address the informational needs of adults, and especially those of women who remain relatively isolated in their communities.

The one Dutch language print source that more people read was free newspapers. Perhaps more door-to-door daily delivery would encourage reading of community and national news. That might work particularly well if summaries of the day's news were included in simplified Dutch with a translation guide provided in Turkish for more difficult words. In Belgium, ad sheets also could introduce news at little cost and high value as a public service. The Flemish regional newspaper, *Gazet van Antwerpen* (circulating in Antwerp and surroundings), makes a considerable effort to insert full-page illustrations with text produced collaboratively between journalists and designers on important cross-cultural issues. These weekly inserts are intended to bring different generations of ethnic minority groups together to read within the family and link them to the community in which they live. Such strategies seem to be appropriate to encourage minorities with limited language skills to bridge to the larger society.

These are small suggestions. The larger issue is to provide the incentive for ethnic minorities to build social capital through bridging. Linking social capital seems to be the real key to changing this. It must be demonstrated that linking can connect ethnic minorities to resources that could ultimately translate into a better life and allow for full integration – in the two-way sense of the term. Each side tends to view the other in stereotypes or generalizations. Only regular social contact can address that issue.

## Notes

1. Putnam's book was written in 2000, preceding the thrust to interactivity on the internet or Web 2.0.
2. The Belgian respondents came from French- as well as Dutch-speaking Belgium.
3. In Belgium immigration policies are determined by region, so Flanders' immigration policies are different from those enacted in Wallonia.
4. The Alevis are Shia Muslims mostly unrelated to the Shiites in Iran. This group generally does not pray five times a day nor attend prayer services at the mosque. They claim to have been misunderstood and even persecuted in Turkey and this is why so many of them chose to work abroad when the opportunity arose. In Turkey they have been associated with free speech and pro-democracy movements. Many Kurdish people are Alevis. A summary of Alevi beliefs and history can be found at: http://www.uga.edu/islam/alevivanb.html
5. Turks refer to the religious period as Ramazan while other Muslims call it Ramadan.
6. Test of significance only used for understanding of the importance of difference. Because of the small sample size in the Dutch sample, no such tests were applied.
7. Fictitious names are chosen, for privacy-preservation purposes.

## References

ARNEIL, BARBARA 2006 *Diverse Communities: The Problem with Social Capital*, New York: Cambridge University Press

BILLIET, JAAK 2006 'Attitudes towards ethnic minorities in Flanders: changes between 1989 and 2003 and a comparison with the Netherlands', in Leen d'Haenens, Marc Hooghe, Dirk Vanheule and Hasibe Gezduci (eds), *'New' Citizens, New Policies? Developments in Diversity Policy in Canada and Flanders*, Ghent: Academia Press, pp. 35–56

BONFADELLI, HEINZ, BUCHER, PRISKA and PIGA, ANDREA 2007 'Old and new media by ethnic minority youth in Europe. With a special emphasis to Switzerland', *Communications. The European Journal for Communication Research*, vol. 32, no. 2, pp. 141–70

BOURDIEU, PIERRE 1986 'The forms of capital', in John Richardson (ed.), *Handbook for Theory and Research for the Sociology of Education*, New York: Greenwood Press, pp. 241–58

BOUSETTA, HASSAN and JACOBS, DIRK 2006 'Multiculturalism, citizenship and Islam in problematic encounters in Belgium', in Tariq Modood, Anna Triandafyllidou and Ricard Zapata-Barrero (eds), *Multiculturalism, Muslims and Citizenship. A European Approach*, London: Routledge, pp. 23–36

CHEN, RENE and THORSON, ESTHER 2007 'Civic participation by educated immigrant population: examining the effects of media use, personal network and social capital', paper presented to the International Communication Association at the annual meeting, Montreal, Canada

COENDERS, MARCEL, LUBBERS, MARCEL and SCHEEPERS, PEER 2003 *Majorities' Attitudes towards Minorities in European Union Member States. Results from the Standard Eurobarometers 1997–2000–2003*, Report 2 for the European Monitoring Centre on Racism and Xenophobia, Nijmegen: University of Nijmegen

COLEMAN, JAMES 1988 'Social capital in the creation of human capital', *American Journal of Sociology*, vol. 94, pp. S95–S120

COLEMAN, JAMES 1990 *Foundations of Social Theory*, Cambridge, MA: Harvard University Press

D'HAENENS, LEEN, EL SGHIAR, HATIM and GOLASZEWSKI, SOFIE 2010 'Ethnic minorities and the media. Trends in research in the Low Countries with a focus on mechanisms of identification with media contents and functions among Flemish families of Moroccan descent', in Thomass Eberwein and Daniel Müller (eds), *Journalismus und Öffentlichkeit. Eine Profession und ihr gesellschaftlicher Auftrag*, Essen: Stiftung Press-Haus NRZ, pp. 193–209

D'HAENENS, LEEN, KOEMAN, JOYCE and SAEYS, FRIEDA 2007 'Digital citizenship among ethnic minority youths in the Netherlands and Flanders', *New Media & Society*, vol. 9, no. 2, pp. 278–99

ELLISON, NICOLE, STEINFIELD, CHARLES and LAMPE, CLIFF 2007 'The benefits of Facebook "friends": social capital and college students' use of online social network sites', *Journal of Computer-Mediated Communication*, vol. 12, no. 4, pp. 1143–68

ENTZINGER, HAN 2003 'The rise and fall of multiculturalism: The case of the Netherlands', in Christian Joppke and Ewa Morawaska (eds), *Toward Assimilation and Citizenship: Immigrants in Liberal Nation-States*, Basingstoke: Palgrave Macmillan, pp. 59–86

EUROPEAN COMMISSION 2007 *Social Cohesion, Trust and Participation: Social Capital, Social Policy and Social Cohesion in the European Union and Candidate Countries*. Available from: http://ec.europa.eu/employment_social/spsi/docs/social_situation/2007_mon_rep_soc_cap.pdf [accessed 3 November 2011]

GRAMSCI, ANTONIO 1971 *Selections from the Prison Notebooks*, New York: International Relations

GÜNTÜRK, REYHAN 1999 'Mediennutzung der Migranten – Mediale Isolation?' [Media use by migrants – media isolation?], in Christoph Butterwegge, Gudrun Hentges and Fatma Sarigöz (eds), *Medien und multikulturelle Gesellschaft*, Opladen: Westdeutscher Verlag, pp. 136–43

HAFEZ, KAI 2002 *Türkische Mediennutzung in Deutschland: Hemmnis oder chance der gesellschaftlichen Integration? Eine qualitative Studie im Auftrag des Presse- und Informationsamtes der Bundesregierung* [Turkish media use in Germany: barrier or chance to social integration?], Hamburg: Deutsches Orient-Institut

HUYSMANS, FRANK and DE HAAN, JOS 2008 'Dagbladen, televisie en internet' [Newspapers, television and the internet', in Andries van den Broeck and Saskia Keuzenkamp (eds), *Het Dagelijkse Leven van Allochtone Stedelingen* [*The Daily Life of Minority City Dwellers*], The Hague: The Netherlands Social Cultural Planning Office, pp. 125–48

KOOPMANS, RUUD 2006 'Trade-offs between equality and difference: The crisis of Dutch multiculturalism in cross-national perspective', *Journal of Ethnic and Migration Studies*, vol. 8, no. 3, pp. 1–30

OGAN, CHRISTINE 2001 *Communication and Identity in Diaspora. Turkish Migrants in Amsterdam and their Use of Media*, Lanham, MD: Lexington Books

PEETERS, ALLERD and D'HAENENS, LEEN 2005 'Bridging or bonding? Relationships between integration and media use among ethnic minorities in the Netherlands', *Communications: The European Journal for Communication Research*, vol. 30, no. 2, pp. 201–31

PROCOPIO, CLAIRE and PROCOPIO, STEVEN 2007 'Did you know what it means to miss New Orleans? Internet communication, geographic community, and social capital in crisis', *Journal of Applied Communication*, vol. 35, no. 1, pp. 67–87

PUTNAM, ROBERT 2000 *Bowling Alone: The Collapse and Revival of American Community*, New York: Simon & Schuster

VASTA, ELLIE 2007 'From ethnic minorities to ethnic majority policy: multiculturalism and the shift to assimilationism in the Netherlands', *Ethnic and Racial Studies*, vol. 30, no. 5, pp. 713–40

WEISS, HANS-JÜRGEN and TREBBE, JOACHIM 2001 Mediennutzung und Integration der türkischen Bevölkerung in Deutschland. Ergebnisse einer Umfrage des Presse- und

Informationsamtes der Bundesregierung [Media use and integration of Turkish people in Germany. Results of a survey by the Federal Press and Information Office]

# Intersectionality and mediated cultural production in a globalized post-colonial world

Isabelle Rigoni

**Abstract**
   This paper aims to demonstrate how intersectionality provides an important conceptual tool to analyse practices of cultural production in ethnic minority media. In the context of the digital age, media are increasingly central as systems of representation of identity, culture and community. However, research examining how ethnic minority media become engaged in struggles of power is rare. Few works have paid attention to the ways in which race and gender operate in tandem to produce and maintain the unequal distribution of power in the mediascape of countries of post-colonial immigration. This paper juxtaposes gender studies and ethnic studies in order to analyse the representation of gender in ethnic media, with a particular focus on journalistic practices.

Our dawning millenium is characterized by three intertwined phenomena: generalized human mobility, unprecedented boost of communication and a proliferation of minority cultures. Mediated technology challenges literature devoted to the study of migration and ethnicity based on the paradigm of *double absence* (Sayad 1999). Analyses of migration based on a series of fractures and binary oppositions (mobile/non-mobile, here/there, absent/present, centre/periphery) described as inherent to migrants and ethnic groups do not fully capture these groups' cultural realities. Information and communication technologies (ICT) have played a particularly important role in enabling new cultural practices and sustaining multiple connections across transnational communities. The media especially become major actors when dealing with identity construction as they provide the primary systems for circulating information and organizing knowledge about 'us' and 'others'. Established scholarship has demonstrated the central role of the media in the development of national narratives (Gellner 1983; Noiriel 2007) and in the construction of imagined (national and transnational) communities (Hobsbawm 1990; Anderson 1991; Appadurai 1997). The role of ethnic media has been discussed as a specific field where identities and bounded communities are reinvented around shared practices of media consumption (Georgiou 2006; Bailey, Georgiou and Harindranath 2007; Titley 2008). Recent developments in the field of ethnic media studies helped to understand that the orientation and production of ethnic minority media must ultimately be understood within a transnational framework that takes into consideration the diversification of information flows, strengthening of diasporic identities and advancement of parallel-mediated systems of self-representation (Rigoni 2010b; Rigoni, Berthomière and Hily 2010). Most notably, this literature has also helped to recognize new trends in European public spheres through the development of diverse media environments, especially through ethnic and diasporic media in and across countries of post-colonial immigration.

This paper intends to contribute to debates on intersectionality as a conceptual tool for analysing forms and practices of media production associated with claims in the areas of ethnic/religious, cosmopolitan/ diversity and citizenship/anti-discrimination issues. The paper looks at a number of minority media, stressing both their role in supporting hegemonic ideologies of racial and gender stratification but also in challenging these systems through politics of resistance. Using theories of intersectionality, I examine the role of ethnic media production in imagining and mobilizing new communities of belonging. I demonstrate that ethnic media production represents an important area of analysis as it allows us to examine new citizenship practices taking into consideration the 'feel' of citizenship (Couldry 2006), as well as the ability of media actors to bridge the difference between ethnic, gender and class divides. Empirically, the paper focuses on the growing contribution of women in European ethnic media production, management and journalistic output. In the first part of this paper, I argue that theories of intersectionality provide an important analytical and conceptual tool for enabling us to understand gender, race and class as dimensions of social identities in transition, especially as reflected in the media. The second part focuses on journalism practice and the ways in which it often reproduces racial and gender divisions within the media. The paper concludes by reflecting on the contradictions associated with the representation of women in ethnic media production and its potential for the emancipation of ethnic minorities, especially ethnic minority women.

**Exploring intertwined social categories in mediated identities**

Intersectionality provides an important framework for the analysis of complex interactions that shape relations of domination and resistance among migrant and ethnic actors, especially women. Intersectionality brings a fresh perspective on minority groups and serves as a theoretical framework for empirical research that analyses the representation and mobilization of cultural minorities in the media. Intersectionality theories bring women to the fore and gender and class into play in understanding the intersecting dimensions of inequality and discrimination that are constitutive of post-colonial state–citizen relations (Rooney 2007).

Aspects of the intersectionality analysis are present whenever two or more social categories are analysed in relation to power and subordination (gender and class, gender and race, class and sexual preferences, etc.). These 'axes of difference' (Klinger and Knapp 2005) do not always 'work' in the same way. They can be symmetrical or one can predominate, and they may find themselves in situations of hierarchy, interbreed or they may represent each other. The concept of intersectionality is used as an analytical tool to explore how various categories of power asymmetries interact in the construction of subjectivity and material conditions of subjects, and thereby contribute to social exclusion and political injustice (Crenshaw 1994). The idea of intersectionality is rooted in several traditions including postmodern feminist theory, post-colonial theory, black feminism and queer theory. As shown by McCall (2005), an emerging interest in intersectionality can be explained by the critique of research based on gender or on ethnicity, which has not taken into account the points of intersection between these different categories. 'Feminists' have somewhat neglected these intersections at first, mainly because of the complexity of relationships of domination experienced by migrant women. They stood in contrast to a singular focus on gender relations as the ultimate relations of domination (Golub, Morokvasic and Quiminal 1997). In the debate about the Islamic headscarves and *niqab* in France and other European countries, it is not uncommon to hear some feminists still defending this kind of analysis.

Unlike some hegemonic feminist streams, since the 1970s, black feminists in the USA have initiated research at the intersection of the categories of gender, race and class. Developing a 'womanist' approach, they aim to demonstrate that women are not all 'white'. Bell hooks calls to deconstruct the category 'woman' as universal and critically examines the hegemonic tendencies of white and middle-class women that focus on claims related to both their 'race' and class (Poiret 2005). In Britain, the feminist re-conceptualization of power as operative within the private sphere as well as the public domain forced cultural studies to rethink its understanding of how hegemony was secured and exercised (Lennox; Franklin, Lury and Stacey 1991), provoking a saving 'rupture' (Hall 1992, p. 282). After that, many studies appeared under the rubric of feminist cultural studies (Shiach 1999). Later on, intersectionality became embraced of queer ambitions to trouble identity demarcations (Butler 1990) and to intensify the analysis of complexity, hybridity, diversity and transformation.These are all conceptualizations devised to help understand the fluidity and/ or stability of identity, subjectification and subject positioning.

In recent years, reflection on the intertwining of power relations has grown increasingly complex. Issues articulating gender and nation, religion and/or skin colour have developed a respectful field of reflection on the intertwining relationships of power (concepts of intersectionality, consubstantiality, globality, post-coloniality) that draws from the contours of an 'epistemology of domination' (Dorlin 2009). More than twenty years after intersectionality was coined by Crenshaw in 1989, the concept has attracted attention in international feminist debates, as it crystallizes many epistemological questions. On the one hand, in several recent conferences, European and American gender studies scholars have discussed the transatlantic travelling of intersectionality, wondering what problems arise with the translation and accommodation of this concept in a transnational context. Intersectionality is considered as a travelling concept (Hemmings and Kaloski), whose design has evolved in different phases of its reception within different academic cultures.

As intersectionality has become internationalized, it has developed forms appropriate to new national and regional settings. Transmuting an approach originally focused on the Anglo-American contexts into a method with a somewhat different focus, intersectionality currently reflects on particular conditions in other countries of the global North and global South. These conceptual adjustments were connected to multiple social movement struggles. Rather than a comprehensive picture that would take too long to deliver here, I mention only two illustrative examples from this literature. Knapp (2006) refers to the impossibility of using the term 'race' in an affirmative and descriptive way in German-speaking countries. Debates are similar in French-speaking countries. There is also a diversity of approaches and designations: in France, Kergoat (2009) prefers the concept of consubstantiality. In this increasingly diverse context, how can we develop an analytical framework across national, regional and cultural borders, while keeping up a politics of location? Several recent analyses have stressed the main tension points in contemporary theorizations of intersectionality and have proposed that the theorectical scope of the concept has broadened (Davis 2008; Bilge 2009). Besides difference, the approaches that can be grouped under the label 'intersectional research' all share the idea that the various social categories of difference are interdependent. Each object of study must be questioned according to the constellation of these categories, depending on the phenomenon of overlapping and interference occurring between them. For the contemporary context, the main points of intersection are 'race', 'economic and social status', and 'gender'. In analysing the various forms of social differentiation and inequality, the buzzword of intersectionality (Davis 2008) suggests that we need to analyse the social and cultural issues together as they relate to actors, institutions and society.

Gender, race and class representations in the media are still relatively under-studied. The present discussion aims to shed light onto the relationship between sociocultural categories and identity in European mediaspaces. I particularly draw on the work of Yuval-Davis, Anthias and Lykke who study the ways in which sociocultural categories change into overlapping ('intra-act') categories, and how different systems of oppression are mutually constructed (Anthias and Yuval-Davis 1993; Yuval-Davis 2006, forthcoming). Here, I focus on the intersection between different social categories in order to understand the position of ethnic media actors and relations of domination in the global society, as well as their vision and awareness of systems of domination. Intersectionality is closely linked to the postmodern condition and the recognition of multidimensional identities, which are in flux and constructed through processes of hybridity and the fragmentation of spaces of belonging.

Attempts to implement this multidimensional approach based on empirical data have actually been rather few in the case of ethnic media. Yet, it is through the stories of minorities themselves that it is possible to understand how the different relations of domination are realized. In analyses of the space of self-representation among minorities, often singular categorical approaches have been reproduced. Such approaches have reaffirmed bounded identity groups rather than analysing the conditions for emergence, reproduction, contestation and transformation of hierarchies related with systems of representation. Drawing on my own and others' fieldwork, I use the intersectionality framework in the analysis of transcultural and transnational processes related to mediated identities. Within this theoretical framework, I propose to analyse the extent to which ethnic minorities' participation in the media reflects the reproduction and challenges to power relations associated with gender, race and class.

## Gendered representations in ethnic media's journalistic practices

Testing theories of intersectionality, this part focuses on media as racially structured and organized, and ethnic media in particular as gendered organizations. As identified in some mainstream media, the trend towards feminization of journalism is widespread, not only in numerical terms, but also in terms of the division of power. I am here exploring whether the glass ceiling and restricted access for women to high positions and prestigious informational fields also hold true in the ethnic media industry. Can we identify areas assigned to the 'feminine' and 'masculine' ethnic media actors? Are gender, race and class relations experienced differently among ethnic media compared to mainstream media? This section intends to provide preliminary analysis using both my own ethnographic research with Muslim media in France, Germany and the UK,[1] my work for Panos Paris Institute in the framework on the European project Mediam'Rad on diversity media[2] and the research conducted under my sypervision within the European project Minority Media.[3]

Questions about the limited presence of ethnic minorities in the mainstream media and of women – ethnic minority and non-ethnic minority – in media decision-making positions are widely relevant in contemporary Europe. As we observed in our study, for ethnic minority women, restrictions to mainstream media are even higher compared to their male counterparts. It is thus no coincidence that we find women in prominent roles as editors and managers of ethnic media much more often than in the case of mainstream media. Cossée (2010) has discussed cases of powerful career women in the production of Roma media in Spain and Hungary. In France, most ethnic women's magazines have been created by women: from *Amina* in the mid-1970s to *Shenka, Kissina, Miss Ebene, Couleur Métiss, Pilibo Mag, Chocolate, Divas*, all dedicated to black women; *Gazelle* and *Yasmina* for Maghrebi women; and *Hawwa* for a Muslim audience. Some of these women have a strong academic background, active presence in the public sphere and thus cultural capital associated with a middle-class identity. Their professional presence reflects a trend reported by two journalists in the Muslim monthly *Q-News* (Ahmad and Tyrer 2005, p. 3):

> Emerging statistics show numbers of Muslim women in university out-weighing Muslim men, and marrying ages among degree-educated Muslim women are rising.... They challenge the "married as soon as possible" stereotypes and are functions of a wider emerging culture of university entry....These women play an important role in paving the way for younger siblings and for other women in their families and communities.

Although this group reflects the growing visibility of women who challenge patriarchal roles within the domestic sphere, the community, educational institutions and as a consequence in ethnic media, there is also a distinct and rather different group of women involved in ethnic media in France, especially as volunteer journalists. These women as less educated, they work at home or have no regular employment. The case of Myriama Youbi, regular freelancer for the Maghrebi French women's monthly *Gazelle*, is one among many within this group. A graduate, she works part time as a specialist organizer and providing academic support to other members of her community. The rest of her time is devoted to her children and to writing articles for the women's magazine *Gazelle*. For her, as for many of her female peers in ethnic media, the journalistic mission is akin to a community spirit of sharing, transmitting a sense of values and exchanging common experiences associated with ethnicity, gender and, to some extent, class. Collaborating with media represents an opportunity for expression and encaptulates a desire to communicate with a broader audience her experience and identity as a woman 'between two cultures'.[4]

Even if many women journalists have acquired significant cultural capital through higher education, there are certain restrictions in their professional life that they often mention. First, there is little access for many of them to the mainstream media, partly at least as a result of the glass ceiling and their limited acculturation within the mainsteam media environment. In addition, and within the minority media environment, they still have to constantly (re-)negotiate their place at work and work hierarchies. Whatever type of position they occupy in the media, women journalists often remain torn between the often contradictory obligations of family and work: most of the ones who occupy positions of responsibility are single and without parental responsibilities. Overall, serious inequalities persist in the gendered distribution of professional tasks, as already pointed out in the mainstream media (Djerf-Pierre 2007; Damian, Frisque and Saitta 2010; Löfgren Nilsson 2010). Despite some women's success stories, Minority Media has revealed similar practices in ethnic media. How might we explain the reproduction of these inequalities?

In analysing our findings through the lens of intersectionality, we can record two processes that are essentially taking place and that restrict equal representation among female and male professionals in ethnic media. The first is associated with horizontal segregation and concerns the logics of distribution of women and men in different sectors, specialities and journalistic skills. As van Zoonen (1998) writes on gendered media production in mainstream media, in this case as well we can see mechanisms that lead to horizontal segregation and its reproduction, despite the increased number of women journalists, and in some cases, their editorial responsibilities (Cossée 2010; Rigoni 2010a). What we have observed in our work and recorded among our participants is both a gender-typing inside newsrooms in terms of tasks, functions, assignment of post and positions, as well as the production of collective meanings of gender through gendered symbolism works in the newsroom. In a number of media, we observed women working as freelancers, recruited as assistants or relegated to the role of the presenter. Carmen Diop, editor of a female black newsmagazine, was appearing on the masthead as an editorial coordinator whereas her counterpart, male and white, was presented as director of information: a kind of summons to female and male functions (interview, March 2010). Daily work, action and language in the newsrooms are also interpreted as being feminine or masculine. This becomes apparent, for example, when quite often women journalists are assigned soft news while hard news is entrusted to their male colleagues. Women journalists are often expected to cover subjects associated with the private sphere and caring, while their male counterparts represent the first point of reference when political and public issues are assigned.

Those ethnic media that give a rewarding place to women have also undergone changes related to a so-called female sensibility: 'female' topics are added, matters associated with the private sphere are more often addressed, and the design of the magazine changes accordingly to reflect the recognition of these media as more egalitarian spaces of representation. The former British Muslim media *Q-News* changed when a woman editor took control:

> The magazine became younger, more positive and more feminine! [laughs] I've added nice colours, you know, I think women are more concerned about appearance. I worried about the magazine. I put pictures on the cover and included powerful images... Fuad Nahdi [previous editor in chief] was very "get the news out there", he had a very different approach. (interview with Shagufta Yaqub, 19 June 2002)

Similarly, *Q-News* added new sections on health, gender relations, sexuality, child rearing, as did other magazines headed by women, like *Hawwa* in France.

Another point to note is that the diversity of both specialization strategies (in terms of sectors, themes, skills) and of relations to sources was developed by women journalists. These are often constructed as systems of control. This diversity may hold true for socially constructed feminine agendas but also, and most importantly, when women are expected to play on and/or mobilize gender stereotypes widely shared by sources, male colleagues, the editors and the media corporations themselves.

The second process, vertical segregation, relates to the logic of inclusion in and exclusion from positions of power in the newsroom. The challenge is to understand the often invisible mechanisms that exclude some groups from positions of power. The assumption of several works is the under-representation of women in (senior) management positions (Gautier 2007; Reiser and Grésy 2008). Implicitly, this research assumes that if more women were in decision-making positions, they would choose more women in positions of responsibility. But various counter-examples, including some observed in our research, show that the individual presence of women in senior positions of responsibility has no significant effect. These examples confirm the deep persistance of systems of stratification that cannot be challenged by individuals alone but that are rooted in general mechanisms of the media industry. One such mechanism identified by Djerf-Pierre (2007) in the case of Swedish media, is the differenciated social, economic, cultural and professional capital available to men and women in positions of responsibility. The working conditions that make it difficult to reconcile professional and private life represent another mechanism and this has been particularly visible in the case of the minority media women journalists whom we interviewed. Many of them could not manage to reconcile a high position in the media and private life with children. Women in positions of responsibility in the ethnic minority media are often single and childless, even when they come from environments where traditional family values are promoted (e.g. Muslims, Roma).

De Bruin and Ross (2004) explain that in order to avoid sexual harassment that develops subtly or directly, verbally or through body language, in the newsroom of some Afro-Caribbean media, some women choose to maintain a professional distance, which moves them away from centres of decision making. Besides working conditions, expectations in terms of speaking and oral performance represent another mechanism for exclusion from positions of power. Some of our participants have noted that they often become intimitaded by the authoritative presence of their male colleagues and superiors and feel unable to share the same language and sense of confidence. Löfgren Nilsson (2010) highlights 'the dominating gender conversation norm' that encourages direct and affirmative expression used preferentially by men, rather than the interrogative inviting discussion used preferentially by women in the case of Swedish television. Finally, masculine patterns of sociability are another such mechanism. Some of our participants have said that male colleagues socialize around gender-specific spaces that they feel intimated from entering.

In the case of ethnic media, we have occasionally observed a conscious desire among editors, managers and journalists to break the glass ceiling that is prominent in mainsteam media and that often excludes minorities and women. This is particularly the case with ethnic media that identify as alternative media. Some of the media we have studied, for instance, organized self-managed systems of childcare to allow greater participation of women. In a context of the growing participation of women in ethnic media, some have gained a high level of responsibilities and have thus contributed to change gender representation in default of gender relations. Elsewhere I have described the role of leading Muslim women journalists in some Muslim media in Britain, France and Spain (Rigoni 2009). Some of them have accessed prominent roles as heads of printed and online magazines (*Trends, Emel, Q-News, Hawwa, Oumma pour Elle* with its blog *Hijab and the City*), newsreaders and programme producers (on *Islam Channel, Radio Faza, Radio Whitechapel Mosque*). Within ethnic media that bring together an increased number of women, the general theme of interpersonal relationships between men and women is discussed with greater regularity, alongside the theme of inter-ethnic relations. While some women we interviewed mentioned the difficulties they have faced in finding a place in the mainstream media, their strong commitment to and participation in ethnic media is the result of a personal choice often closely tied to either political, social or religious activism. This activism seeks to improve ethnic as well as gender relations within the community group and mainstream society. In such cases, their involvement reflects an attempt to combine gender equality, engagement in the public arena and defence of minority rights. Ethnicity and gender become radically intertwined.

Also, several ethnic media are specifically designed by and for women. In recent immigration countries, like Spain, media outlets for migrant women are going through a process of growth and initial market consolidation, despite the current economic crisis that strongly affects the media sector and in particular ethnic media. Do these women's ethnic media offer alternative representations of gender and race relations? The handful of studies on media outlets for women of ethnic minority background shows that they are constantly contributing to the emergence of strong and positive images of women. In her study on the discourse, representation and images of Latin American immigrant women in ethnic newspapers in the Spanish Basque country, Mendieta (forthcoming) shows that 'immigrant women have a greater representation as active protagonists or subjects of their own stories, not as victims of discrimination, as domestic workers, or as mothers or wives.' These women's magazines cover stories on migrant women as leading political and social activists, academics or white-collar professionals. A greater representation of migrant women allows these publications to promote different topics than those covered in mainstream media, as well as in 'gender-blind' ethnic media. In her study on the women's French black magazine *Brune*, Sassoon (forthcoming) argues that it 'opens an alternative space of visibility to a racialised norm of feminity'. *Brune* fights its way against the dominant and normative vision of black beauty offering a variety of role models, rejecting advertisements for skin-whitening products and urging readers not to imitate the 'European canons of beauty'. Sassoon stresses that the magazine condemns vehemently both patriarcal society and the brutal version of capitalism it sees as generating inequalities. The interlocking systems of domination, with a transnational dimension, steps out in this invective on the current financial crisis (Sassoon forthcoming):

> This tragedy reaches the wallet of the poorest and causes needless additional suffering among the peoples of the South... this should force us today to say stop! Yes, women now say stop to men! It is high time to find ways of capitalism-friendly standards and rules in the service of humanity. (translated from French by author)

In this example, women are directly encouraged to act to restore balance in a broken system led by men. More generally, several case studies show that dimensions related to gender, class and race influence information processing and choice of themes. They appear alternatively or simultaneously, through a feminist and anti-racist position, critical of the abuses of the capitalist system, particularly in terms of sustaining inequalities between the global North and South.

Last but not least, women have contributed to the renewal of ethnic media discourse related to the fight against discrimination. They have particularly contributed to highlighting anti-discrimination, especially in addressing their own double discrimination – as women in a patriarchal society and as migrants and/or members of ethnic minorities. Alam (2005, p. 3), editor-in-chief of one of the leading British Muslim magazines, *Q-News*, illustrates this position:

> Islam "liberates" women, but for how long will we hide the very real inequalities in our communities, behind this cliché? I love my hijab, but how can I go along with the wishful-thinking that hijabis are automatically de-sexualised just because they cover their hair? How can I feign ignorance of the fact that the hijab has, sadly, not proven to be a barrier to teenage pregnancy or drug and alcohol abuse, so rife in Pakistani and Bengladeshi communities in Britain?[5]

For this young Muslim journalist, as for others, faith liberates the feminine 'individuality' but cannot hide the fact that women are still victims of flagrant inequalities, both within and outside their community.

## Conclusion

In this paper I aimed to highlight some of the lessons learned in applying theories of intersectionality to the analysis of ethnic media. These approaches allow us to understand the realities of ethnic media production not as a separate and single-dimensional sphere of community representation but also as an agonistic space. Intersectionality helps to better understand the role of ethnic media, not only for intra-community life but also for intercultural dialogue and gender relations within the media sector and in society. Theories related to the interlocking system of domination allows us to understand how people struggle with multiple identities, while at the same time being caught within hegemonic systems of gender and racial stratification. Reading ethnic media in the light of theories of intersectionality allows us to apprehend not only race relations but also gender relations within them. While focusing on gender representation within journalism, I aimed to underline the gendering processes in ethnic minority media production and how it (re)produces inequalities around gender.

What I also argue is that research on ethnic media in itself contributes to advancing debates on intersectionality. Indeed, ethnic media appear as a promising field to think about the intricacy of ethnicity, gender and class relations of domination. Since the globalization of migration and of information flows and the growing use of ICT among ethnic minorities, ethnic media have gained a visible presence – alongside other community organizations – in the construction of identity and community. Because they help to strengthen community identity by maintaining or reinventing collective memory – what Husband (1994) called the 'media invented heritage' – ethnic media find themselves caught between traditional and progressing systems of race and gender relations. Analysing ethnic media in this way allows us to show and analyse resistance but also the various forms of adherence of individuals and minority groups to the hegemonic ideology on the place of ethnic minorities within society and the role of women and men in the public sphere.

As our research shows, ethnic media do not necessarily develop sensitivities that recognize the interweaving of gender, class and race systems of domination. Several just reproduce them. As Diop (forthcoming) points out, gender remains an obscured and an obscuring element in women's progress in ethnic media. Often representation of women in ethnic media remains widely stereotyped. However, these media appear as a niche with significant potential to challenge racialized inequalities, especially as their potentiality of fairer representation lies on their own intertwining of experiences of marginalization associated with gender, class and generation.

## Acknowledgements

I particularly thank Myria Georgiou for her work on editing the text, and my colleague Daniel Alexander Gordon for his careful reading of the English version of my paper.

## Notes

1. I conducted qualitative research on Muslim media at the Centre for Research in Ethnic Relations (CRER), University of Warwick (2001–3), at the Goethe Institute in Berlin (2004–5) and at MIGRINTER-CNRS in Poitiers (2006–10). I particularly refer in this paper to semi-structured interviews made at *Q-News*, *The Muslim News*, *Die Islamische Zeitung* and *Salam News*.
2. Mediam'Rad is a European project conducted in 2005–8 on diversity in the media in France, Italy and the Netherlands. The project leader was Panos Paris Institute. Mediam'Rad implemented various activities of research action, some of which I have been involved in, including the first prize of 'diversity media' in 2007; meetings between diversity media and mainstream media to promote inter-cultural dialogue; a directory on 'diversity media'; and a report on 'diversity media' content in terms of information processing.
3. Minority Media is a Marie Curie Excellence Team funded by the EU (2006–10) and hosted by the research centre MIGRINTER at the University of Poitiers (France). The research focused on the study of ethnic minority media in a comparative and multi-disciplinary perspective (www.irigoni.blogspot.com). Fieldwork has been conducted in eight European countries: France, Germany, Hungary, Italy, the Netherlands, Spain, Turkey and the UK.
5. Myriama Youbi, 'D'origine maghrébine', *Gazelle*, décembre/janvier 2005. Interview, January 2007, Paris.

## References

AHMAD, FAUZIA and TYRER, IMRAN 2005 *Q-News*, 364, November, p. 3
ALAM, FAREENA 2005 'Editorial', *Q-News*, 361, March
ANDERSON, BENEDICT 1991 *Imagined Communities*, New York: Verso
ANTHIAS, FLOYA and YUVAL-DAVIS, NIRA 1993 *Racialized Boundaries: Race, Nation, Gender, Colour and Class and the Anti-Racist Struggle*, London: Routledge
APPADURAI, ARJUN 1997 *Modernity at Large: Cultural Dimensions of Globalization*, Minneapolis, MN: University of Minnesota Press
BAILEY, OLGA G., GEORGIOU, MYRIA and HARINDRANATH, RAMASWAMI (eds) 2007 *Transnational Lives and the Media: Reimagining Diasporas*, Basingstoke: Palgrave
BAUBÖCK, RAINER (ed.) 1994 *From Alien to Citizens: Redefining the Status of Immigrants in Europe*, Aldershot: Avebury
BECK, ULRICH 2006 *Cosmopolitan Vision*, Cambridge, MA: Polity Press
BILGE, SIRMA 2009 'Théorisations féministes de l'intersectionnalité', *Diogène*, no. 225, janvier, pp. 70–88.
BUTLER, JUDITH 1990 *Gender Trouble: Feminism and the Subversion of Identity*, London: Routledge

CHAMBERS, DEBORAH, STEINER, LINDA and FLEMING, CAROLE 2004 *Women and Journalism*, London: Routledge
COSSÉE, CLAIRE 2010 'Médias tsiganes en France et en Hongrie: re-présentation de soi dans l'espace public', Revue européenne des migrations internationales, Special issue 'Les médias des minorités ethniques'. *Représenter l'identité collective sur la scène publique'*, vol. 26, no. 1, pp.57–78
COULDRY, NICK 2006 'Culture and citizenship. The missing link?', *European Journal of Cultural Studies*, vol. 9, no. 3, pp. 321–39
CRENSHAW, KIMBERLE 1989 *'Demarginalizing the Intersection of Race and Sex: A Black Feminist Critique of Antidiscrimination Doctrine, Feminist Theory and Antiracist Politics'*, University of Chicago Legal Forum, pp.139–67
CRENSHAW, KIMBERLÉ 1994 'Intersectionality and identity politics: learning from violence against women of color', in *Martha Albertson Fineman and Rixanne Mykitiuk, The Public Nature of Private Violence*, London: Routledge, pp.178–93
DAMIAN, BEATRICE (ed.), FRISQUE, CEGOLENE and SAITTA, EUGÉNIE 2010 *Le journalisme au féminin: assignations, inventions et stratégies*, Rennes: Presses Universitaires de Rennes
DAVIS, KATHY 2008 'Intersectionality as buzzword', *Feminist Theory*, vol. 9, no. 1, pp. 67–85
DE BRUIN, MARJAN and ROSS, KAREN (eds) 2004 *Gender and Newsroom Cultures. Identities at Work*, Cresskill: Hampton Press
DIMINESCU, DANA 2007 *Study on Social Computing and Immigrants and Ethnic Minorities: Usage Trends and Implications*, Paris: Fondation de la Maison des Sciences de l'Homme
DIOP, CARMEN forthcoming 'Les femmes noires diplômées dans l'espace médiatique francophone', in Claire Cossée, Laura Navarro Garcia, Isabelle Rigoni and Eugénie Saitta (eds), *Rapports genrés et imbrication des systèmes de domination dans les médias des minorités*, Paris: Petra, coll. IntersectionS
DJERF-PIERRE, MONIKA 2007 'The gender of journalism. the structure and logic of the field in the twentieth century', *Nordicom Review*, Jubilee Issue, pp. 81–104
DORLIN, ELSA (ed.) 2009 'Sexe, race, classe'. *Pour une épistémologie de la domination*, Paris: PUF
ESTRADA CARVALHAIS, ISABEL 2007 'The cosmopolitan language of the state', *European Journal of Social Theory*, vol. 10, no. 1, pp. 99–111
FRACHON, CLAIRE and SASSOON, VIRGINIE (eds) 2009 *Media and Cultural Diversity in Europe and North America*, Paris: Karthala/Institut Panos Paris
FRANKLIN, SARAH, LURY, CELIA and STACEY, JACKIE (eds) 1991 *Off Centre: Feminism and Cultural Studies*, London: Routledge
GAUTIER, GISELE 2007 *Femmes et hommes dans les médias, Rapport d'activité de la délégation aux droits des femmes et à l'égalité des chances entre hommes et femmes au Paris: Sénat*
GELLNER, ERNEST 1983 *Nations and Nationalism*, Oxford: Blackwell
GEORGIOU, MYRIA 2006 *Diaspora, Identity and the Media: Diasporic Transnationalism and Mediated Spatialities*, New York: Hampton Press
GOLUB, ANNE, MOROKVASIC, MIRJANA and QUIMINAL, CATHERINE 1997 'Évolution de la production des connaissances sur les femmes immigrées en France et en Europe', *Migrations Société*, vol. 9, no. 52, juillet, pp. 19–36.
HABERMAS, JÜRGEN 1998 *The Inclusion of the Other: Studies in Political Theory*, Cambridge, MA: MIT Press
HALL, STUART 1992 'Cultural studies and its theoretical legacies', in Lawrence Grossberg, Cary Nelson and Paula Treichler (eds), *Cultural Studies*, London: Routledge, pp. 277–86
HEMMINGS, CLARE and KALOSKI, ANN (eds) TravellingConcepts.net, York, Raw Nerve Books, http://www.rawnervebooks.co.uk/travellingconcepts.html [Accessed 14 April 2010]

HOBSBAWM, ERIK 1990 *Nations and Nationalism since 1780: Programme, Myth, Reality*, Cambridge, MA: Cambridge University Press
HUSBAND, CHARLES 1994 *A Richer Vision: The Development of Ethnic Minority Media in Western Democracies*, Paris: UNESCO
HUTCHINGS, KIMBERLY and DANNREUTHER, ROLAND 1998 *Cosmopolitan Citizenship*, New York: Palgrave Macmillan
―――― 2001 'Media and the public sphere in multi-ethnic societies', in Simon Cottle (ed.), *Ethnic Minorities and the Media*, Maidenhead: Open University Press
KASTORYANO, RIVA 1998 *Quelle identité pour l'Europe? Le multiculturalisme à l'épreuve*, Paris: Presses de Science Po
KERGOAT, DANIELE 2009 'Dynamique et consubstantialité des rapports sociaux', in Elsa Dorlin (ed.), *Sexe, race, classe. Pour une épistémologie de la domination*, Paris: PUF
KLINGER, CORNELIA and KNAPP, GUDRUN-AXELI 2005 *'Achsen der Ungleichheit – Achsen der Differenz. Verhältnisbestimmungen von Klasse, Geschlecht, "Rasse"/Ethnizität'*, Transit. *Europäische Revue*, no. 29, Juli
KNAPP, GUDRUN-AXELI 2006 *'"Intersectionality": Feministische Perspektiven auf Ungleichheit und Differenz im gesellschaftlichen Transformationsprozeß'*, lecture at the international conference on Paradoxes in Gender Relations, Bern University
KNUDSEN, SUSANNE V. 1995 'Intersectionality. A theoretical inspiration in the analysis of minority cultures and identities in textbooks', paper presented at the conference Theory: Caught in the Web or Lost in the Textbook, Caen: France
LENNOX, SARA 'Feminism and cultural studies', Available from: http://daadcenter.wisc.edu/events/2005/Lennox-cultural&feminism.pdf [Accessed 9 October 2011]
LICOPPE, CHRISTIAN 2002 "Sociabilité et technologies de communication'. Deux modalités d'entretien des liens interpersonnels dans le contexte du déploiement des dispositifs de communication mobiles', *Réseaux*, no. 1123, pp. 172–210
LÖFGREN NILSSON, MONICA 2010 'Thinkings and doings of gender. Gendering processes in Swedish television news production', *Journalism Practice*, vol. 4, no. 1, pp. 1–16
MCCALL, LESLIE 2005 "The complexity of intersectionality", *Signs: Journal of Women in Culture and Society*, vol. 3, no. 3, pp. 1771–800
MARCHETTI, DOMINIQUE and RUELLAN, DENIS 2001 *Devenir journalistes. Sociologie de l'entrée sur le marché du travail*, Paris: La Documentation française
MENDIETA, ANA FORTHCOMING "Discours, représentation et images des immigrantes latino-américaines dans les journaux des minorités ethniques au Pays basque" in Claire Cossée, Laura Navarro Garcia, Isabelle Rigoni and Eugénie Saitta (eds), *Rapports genrés et imbrication des systèmes de domination dans les médias des minorités*, Paris: Petra, coll. IntersectionS
NEDELCU, MIHAELA 2009 'Le migrant online'. *Nouveaux modèles migratoires à l'ère du numérique*, Paris: L'Harmattan
NOIRIEL, GERARD 2007 *A quoi sert l'identité nationale*, Paris: Agone
POIRET, CHRISTIAN 2005 "Articuler les rapports de sexe, de classe et interethniques. Quelques enseignements du débat nord-américain", *Revue européenne des migrations internationales, n° spécial 'Femmes, genre, migrations, mobilités'*, vol. 21, no. 1, pp. 195–226
PROULX, SERGE 2008 'Des nomades connectés: vivre ensemble à distance', *Hermès*, no. 51, pp. 155–66
REISER, MICHELE and GRÉSY, BRIGITTE 2008 *Rapport sur l'image des femmes dans les médias*, Paris: Commission de réflexion sur l'image des femmes dans les médias
REVILLARD, ANNE and DE VERDALLE, LAURE 2006 "'Faire" le genre, la race et la classe. Introduction à la traduction de "Doing Difference"', *Terrains & travaux*, no. 10, janvier
RIGONI, ISABELLE 2009 'Media and Muslims in Europe', in Jorgen S. Nielsen, Samim Akgönül, Ahmet Alibasic, Brigitte Maréchal, Christian Moe (eds), *Yearbook of Muslims in Europe*, Leiden: Brill, pp. 475–505

RIGONI, ISABELLE 2010a 'Journalisme, militantisme et enjeux des mobilisations solidaires. Genre, religion et classe dans la presse écrite musulmane outre-Manche', in Béatrice Damian, Cégolène Frisque and Eugénie Saitta (eds), *Le journalisme au féminin: assignations, inventions et stratégies*, Rennes: Presses Universitaires de Rennes

RIGONI, ISABELLE (ed.) 2010b 'Migrants, minorités ethniques et Internet. Usages et représentations', *Migrations Société*, vol. 22, no. 132, novembre-décembre pp. 31–176.

RIGONI, ISABELLE, BERTHOMIÈRE, WILLIAM and HILY, MARIE-ANTOINETTE 2010 'Les médias des minorités ethniques. Représenter l'identité collective sur la scène publique', *Revue européenne des migrations internationales*, vol. 26, no. 1, mars pp.7–139 (special issue)

ROONEY, EILISH 2007 'Intersectionality in transition: lessons from Northern Ireland', *Web Journal of Current Legal Issues* [Accessed 14 April 2010]

SASSOON, VIRGINIE forthcoming '*Le magazine* Brune *Magazine, un autre regard sur les femmes noires*', in Claire Cossée, Laura Navarro Garcia, Isabelle Rigoni and Eugénie Saitta (eds), *Rapports genrés et imbrication des systèmes de domination dans les médias des minorités*, Paris: Petra, coll. IntersectionS

SAYAD, ABDELMALEK 1999 *La double absence*, Paris: Seuil

SHIACH, MORAG 1999 *Feminism in Cultural Studies*, Oxford: Oxford University Press

SOYSAL, YASEMIN 1994 *Limits of Citizenship: Migrants and Postnational Membership in Europe*, Chicago, IL: Chicago University Press

STAUNÆS, DORTHE 2003 'Where have all the subjects gone? Bringing together the concepts of intersectionality and subjectification', *NORA*, vol. 11, no. 2, pp. 101–10

TAMBINI, DAMIAN 2001 'Post-national citizenship', *Ethnic and Racial Studies*, vol. 24, no. 2, pp. 195–217

TITLEY, GAVAN 2008 'Media transnationalism in Ireland: an examination of Polish media practices', *Translocations: The Irish Migration, Race and Social Transformation Review*, vol. 3, no. 1, pp. 29–49

TITLEY, GAVAN and LENTIN, ALANA (eds) 2008 *The Politics of Diversity in Europe*, Strasbourg: Council of Europe Publishing

VAN ZOONEN, LIESBET 1998 'One of the girls? Or the changing gender of journalism', in Cynthia Carter, Gill Branston and Stuart Allan (eds), *News, Gender and Power*, London, Routledge, pp. 33–46

YUVAL-DAVIS, NIRA 2006 'Intersectionality and feminist politics', *European Journal of Women's Studies*, vol. 13, no. 3, pp. 193–209

——— forthcoming *Intersectional Politics of Belonging*, London: Sage

# Watching soap opera in the diaspora: cultural proximity or critical proximity?

Myria Georgiou

**Abstract**
This paper focused on an area of transnational Arabic television, which has attracted little scholarly attention: soap operas and their consumption among women in the Arab diaspora. Focus groups with Arab audiences in London revealed the significant role that soap operas play in sustaining a gendered critical and reflexive proximity to the Arab world. The paper shows that soap opera viewing provides female audiences in the diaspora with opportunities to reflect on their own gender identities as distant from hegemonic discourses of gender in their region of origin but as proximate to a moral set of values they associate with this same region. This was especially, but not exclusively, the case with young women born in the diaspora.

The rise and rise of Arabic television has both fascinated and troubled the west. While its transnational appeal is recorded both in research and public debates, the nuances and tensions associated with its consumption are far less understood. Knowing about the success of television networks among audiences is not enough to understand the socio-cultural significance of Arabic transnational television. It is in the close examination of what audiences watch and how they make sense of television within gendered and generational contexts that we can observe its complex cultural role. This paper focuses on Arab women in the diaspora and soap operas, two subjects having received little scholarly attention.

It is tempting to interpret transnational Arabic television's success as a cross-border reaffirmation of the thesis of cultural proximity. In

La Pastina and Straubhaar's words, aspects of cultural proximity 'are purely cultural and linguistic...when migrants continue to have a strong layer of identity linked to their "home" country or culture' (2005, p. 274). Is this the case with dispersed Arab communities? Are diasporic women's identities directly linked to a distant 'home' as if there was an uncut and ever-present umbilical cord connecting the two ends? And is there any evidence demonstrating that diasporic female audiences engage with cultural politics in their region of origin? In order to understand if and under what circumstances diasporic audiences locate themselves close or far away from the Arab region's cultural politics, I examine cultural proximity's relevance within a diasporic gendered context.

Television, and the genre of soap opera in particular, provides a vivid case study. As will be shown, the thesis of cultural proximity is still relevant when it comes to diasporic Arab women's soap opera viewing. Yet, and importantly, it is reincarnated as a critical and reflexive negotiation of proximity and distance. Specifically, I argue that soap opera viewing provides female audiences in the diaspora with opportunities to reflect on their own gender identities as distant from hegemonic discourses of gender in their region of origin but as proximate to a moral set of values they associate with this same region. This is especially the case for young women who have grown up in the diaspora.

Drawing from focus group research in London[1], I locate this discussion at the juxtaposition of research on gendered media consumption as this is informed by the study of diasporic, transnational and Arabic audiences. I discuss empirical findings under three sections. These correspond to the main themes that emerged in participants' discourse when they talk about soap operas, Arabic television and their affiliation with their region of origin[2]: (1) distance; (2) proximity; (3) critical proximity. The theme of distance highlights detachment from the Arab region and its cultural politics. The theme of proximity captures soap operas' emotional and commodity value in supporting a sense of belonging in a transnational community. The theme of critical proximity demonstrates how the sense of distance and of proximity from the Arab region merges into a reflexive realization of its internal contradiction: participants sustain a cultural attachment to the Arab region beyond geographical distance, but keep a distance from its hegemonic representations of gender. Within this theme, I discuss the subgenre of Turkish soap operas, as audiences' engagement with it exemplifies critical proximity. Turkish soap operas and their controversial role in Arabic mediascapes provide participants with opportunities to reflect on what it means to be an Arab, as well as a member of a gendered transnational audience.

## Transnational audiences and soap opera consumption

Studies of media and diaspora, gendered soap opera consumption, and cultural proximity have historically followed parallel routes. Effectively, there has been little cross-fertilization of our understanding of diasporic women's relation to soap operas. Research on diaspora and the media has demonstrated the expansion of communication across transnational diasporic spaces, which can support diasporic identities and communities (Gillespie 1995; Brikenhoff 2009; Karanfil 2009). This research has also contributed to conceptualizations of diaspora as a complex and contradictory condition; diasporic affiliation might persist alongside internal power struggles. As dispersed audiences get access to and consume the same media across space, a sense of commonality is reinforced and even reinvented (Georgiou 2006). Sharing media provides diasporic groups with opportunities to develop common cultural practices and thus, at least momentarily, to surpass internal generational, class and gender divides (Karanfil 2009).

Arabs in London represent a diverse group with the majority originating in the Middle East (Miladi 2006). Previous research, as well as the present study, have recorded a persistent and strong identification of many Arab-speakers in Britain with a group identity (Gillespie 2006; Miladi 2006), in ways similar to those identified by Cohen as key diasporic qualities (1997). These include a strong sense of solidarity towards other Arabs and a group consciousness based on a sense of distinctiveness and a belief in a common fate (ibid.). Identification with the Arab diaspora does not necessarily compete with particular Arab regional or national diasporic affiliations.

As in the case of other diasporic audiences, the one studied here cannot be singularly understood by their *Arabness*. Diasporic audiences occupy different social and cultural spaces (Karanfil 2009). Importantly though, the spread and success of transnational Arabic television provides a significant indicator of the emergence of a powerful Arabic linguistic and cultural mediascape[3]. Kraidy (2010) locates transnational television in the core of Arab modernity. Abu-Lughod (2005), with reference to television in Egypt, demonstrates that it has played a key role in shaping social and political debates on modernity and providing a platform for self-making, especially for women. Both Kraidy and Abu-Lughod locate their analysis of Arabic television within the battlefield of conflicting perceptions of modernity. In his study of Arabic reality shows and the public debates around them, Kraidy argues that 'disputes over reality TV were proxy battles to draw boundaries between reality and image, the masculine and the feminine, the pure and the hybrid, the authentic and the foreign' (2010, p. 15). Arabic audiences in London consume transnational television and find themselves caught in these battles for modernity. At the same time, they constitute an element of western audiences. Thus, their practices need to be understood at the juxtaposition of cultural politics associated with Arabic and with western television[4]. Like for other audiences, television consumption represents an ordinary and banal element of everyday life (Silverstone 1994). Thus, the audience discussed here is not by definition different to other audiences.

Diasporic Arab audiences are on the receiving side of cultural politics in the Arab world, mainly through regular consumption of transnational television. Female participants showed they are well aware of the tensions around modernity and tradition in the Arab world, especially in terms of gender representations. At the same time, they are located outside the region. Their engagement with its cultural politics presents an interesting twist to struggles around the representation of women on the screen and in the public sphere. The interplay between proximity and distance becomes an everyday reality for diaspora; it is about being *with* distant others without being *in* distant places. A sense of distance – and relative 'objectivity' in the form of reflexivity – might be the inevitable result of geography, but it is also a socio-cultural reality associated with living in different places – in this case London – and having multiple identities (Rizvi 2006).

Theorizations of cultural proximity are useful here as they make links between media industries' intensions, systems of distribution and media consumption. The concept was introduced by Straubhaar (1991) to articulate the persistent success of national and regional media products vis-à-vis global products, especially those produced in Hollywood. Cultural proximity links changes in media industries and technologies to cultural, linguistic and historical profiles of audiences. In Straubhaar's definition, cultural proximity refers to 'nationally or locally produced material that is closer to and more reinforcing of traditional identities, based in regional, ethnic, dialect/language, religious, and other elements' (1991, p. 51). Audience preferences are dynamic and relational: they respond to the limitations characterizing national production, to social and historical subnational and supranational differences that influence different groups' media choices (Sinclair 1999) and to state strategies of nearing and distancing (Murji in Qureshi 2007). As put by Qureshi (2007, p. 295): 'Relations and perceptions of distance and proximity are not given but created in processes involving the national state, the media, local authorities and people themselves'.

As La Pastina and Straubhaar argue, shared histories of migration can also trigger interest in programmes originating in geographically distant territories. Soap opera is such a case: 'Melodrama builds on underlying oral structures, formulas and archetypes than can be shared by cultures' (2005, p. 275). In discussing migrant audiences, La Pastina and Straubhaar (2005) talk of transnational continuities in cultural proximity. However, the interlocking of 'closeness and remoteness' (Simmel 1908) remains outside this analysis. While literature on media and diaspora on the other hand has addressed the tensions between origin and diaspora (cf. Gillespie 1995; Georgiou 2006; Qureshi 2007; Kandifil 2009), the conceptual debate remains open: is diaspora contained in the cultural space of its region of origin or is it positioned in a parallel – or even competing – space?

*Soap operas and cultural proximity*

Changes in transnational television challenge the limits of cultural proximity debates, but also of soap opera consumption as a private affair, primarily associated with white western middle-class women. Research which has historically looked at the transnational success of soap opera has focused on three main areas: (1) exploring the role of the genre's circulation in relation to questions of cultural imperialism (Lee 1980; Mattelart, Delcourt and Mattelart 1984); (2) examining gendered patterns of consumption and whether they reaffirm female subordination or emancipation (Abu-Lughod, 2002; Mayer 2003; Abu-Lughod 2005); (3) interrogating (dis-)continuities between migrants and national imagined communities (Liebes and Katz 1990; Burch 2002). Transnationally-oriented research has drawn from long and established research on soap opera, which has primarily been located in the west. Connections between soap opera viewing and female reflection on sexuality (Geraghty 1991), the possibility of making alternative life choices when identifying with soap operas' heroines (Livingstone 1991), and the limits (or expansion) of female silence within patriarchal family structures (Modleski 1982; Brown 1994) have been themes addressed in the analysis of transnational, as well as national audiences. Abu-Lughod (2005) explains how melodrama in Egypt provides a sense of visibility to ordinary people and how progressive values are circulated in its themes. Soap operas support female audiences' sense of individuality, which many of them are deprived of, especially in working-class and rural environments. At the same time, Abu-Lughod argues, ideals of female emancipation on the screen have little relevance to these audiences. This comes as no surprise taking that the life of working-class women in Egypt could not be more different from the life of the urban middle class that produces them. The huge discrepancy between the experiences of audiences and producers which Abu-Lughod describes in the case of Egypt has no parallel to the social experience of most members of Arabic soap opera audiences in London. These audiences are urban and in the case of younger women especially, well educated.

Migrant women's viewing of soap operas has been addressed to some extent in research, primarily in the US. Barrera and Bielby (2001), who studied Latina viewers in the US, argue that telenovelas[5] bridge geographical distance between women and their country of origin. Mayer (2003) suggests that telenovela viewing among young Mexican women in San Antonio challenges male domination in their lives, especially as women take breaks from hectic housework to watch their favourite shows. Such studies recognize the ordinariness and banality of transnational soap opera viewing among migrant women. At the same time, they export to a transnational context some of the limitations of earlier soap opera reception research. For example, they retain an almost exclusive focus on a single social group (i.e. first generation migrant women) and a preference for cases within bounded places. Transnational research, which is open to multi-generational diasporic experiences and disrupted geographies remains marginal.

*Soap operas and gendered Arab audiences*

The relation between gender and soap operas on Arabic television needs to be understood within the context of modernity. Abu-Lughod (2010) explains how feminism has become a contested ideology in Egypt with Islamists gaining ground by resisting it as an instrument of colonial domination. Gender relations have been at the core of many social and political struggles in the Arab region throughout modernity with women often being targeted either as the bastion or a threat to morality. Abu-Lughod's writes about the current advance of 'retraditionalization' ideologies in Egypt, with women finding themselves praised for modesty and for staying at home and criticized for having career aspirations (2010). Kraidy (2010) shows that young men have found some of the conservative Islamist ideas about gender relations attractive at times of rising unemployment and increased public female visibility. Media have played a key role in the struggles for female emancipation, Abu-Lughod writes with reference to Egypt, as television melodrama has become one of the 'technologies for the production of new kinds of selves' (2005, p. 113). While television programmes that challenge hegemonic perceptions of gender identities might not influence people in radical ways, Abu-Lughod (2010) adds, they do reflect processes of modernization.

Soap operas have an established presence on Arabic television. Egyptian and Syrian soap operas have been successful across the Middle East since the 1980s. Some of those series touched sensitive issues, such as rape and stigmatization of women in the Arab world (Hafez 2008). Turkish soap operas, which are dubbed in a colloquial version of Arabic has marked recent developments within the genre and its reception. They have captivated Arabic audiences since 2008, breaking all viewership records. *Noor*[6] became the highest rated show ever (Al Arabiya 2008; *International Herald Tribune* 2010). One of Turkish soap operas' key characteristics, which has since been taken over by Arab 'home grown' productions, is the central presence of beautiful, career-oriented and aware of their sexuality heroines. The representation of emancipated women on the screen has turned into a battlefield, celebrated by audiences and condemned by religious and political conservative leaders (Buccianti 2010).

## Methodology

The paper draws from nine focus group interviews conducted in London over two periods: June 2009 and February 2011. The six focus groups conducted in June 2009 were divided between single gendered adult female and male groups with 6–8 participants each. The focus groups were organized in three age groups: 18–25, 26–45, 46–65. Following the same structure, three additional female focus groups were conducted in February 2011 in order to enrich further our understanding of gendered discourses of media consumption and identity. First and second generation migrants were almost equally represented in the two younger groups. The migrant generation predominated in the 46–65 groups. Most participants originate in the Middle East and all are settled in Britain, though not all have citizenship rights[7]. Class and education background varied with working-class and middle-class participants almost equally represented. This diversity broadly represents the demographic composition of the Arab population in Britain (Miladi 2006). For this study, sample diversity did not present an obstacle but a strength, as its purpose was to record the range of experiences and opinions in relation to transnational television. Participants were chosen based on their self-identification as Arab-speakers[8] and the fact that they all have access to transnational Arabic television. The snowballing technique was used for recruitment. Focus groups were conducted in either or both languages – i.e. Arabic and English – and according to participants' preference.

Questions asked fell within two broad themes: media use and sense of belonging. In the case of both themes, questions were open-ended. Participants were asked questions such as: 'How would you describe yourself?' and 'What did you watch last night?' The research team made no assumptions about the meanings of *Arabness* or of Arabic television. Analysis was inductive and showed that transnational television holds an important role in everyday life and that most participants identified as Arabs[9].

## Watching soap operas in the diaspora

Soap operas on Arabic television proved to be very popular among participants, especially women. Most female participants, no matter their social status, said that they watch some soap operas on Arabic television. Gender, age and education informed the level of reflexive engagement with soap operas with the younger, better-educated women appearing as the most critically engaged. For most participants, soap opera viewing is diverse and transnational. They might watch Turkish soap operas alongside Egyptian and Syrian productions (*musalsalaat*), such as *Bab AlHarrah*[10], as well as British soap operas, such as *Eastenders*, and American ones, such as *Glee* and *Desperate Housewives*. The genre's integration in familial life both captures and reproduces some of the tensions associated with divides along the lines of age, generation and gender, as in the case of other households in western societies (Livingstone 1995). For example, participants of all ages confirm that it is the elderly and male family members who mostly control the family's main television set.

> I watch TV with my husband, he is the boss, he decides on what to watch...When my husband is absent, I am the boss and I choose (Female, 26–45).

> My dad controls the remote control up to about 8 o'clock in the evening. After that he falls asleep and then my mum gets it for the *musalsalaat* [soap operas] (Male, 26–45).

While gender hierarchies are confirmed in these comments, control is always conditional and subject to familial daily life changes. Alongside established routines, many participants describe the temporality of Arabic language soap opera consumption. This is especially the case during Ramadan, when soap opera viewing peaks.

> We are not a big *musalsalaat* family unless it's Ramadan when we call each other from different floors to get down and watch TV (Female, 18–25)

Participants' words did reflect the ideological and cultural diversity of the Arab diaspora and so did the patterns of their use of television. Overall, more selective and individual media use is common among younger men and women:

> Honestly, my grandmother holds the remote control and watches soaps. She doesn't give me a chance to do anything so I go to the

internet to watch whatever I like. When she is not there, I choose whatever I want to watch on TV (Female, 18–25).

With a focus on the negotiation of cultural proximity and distance, the following three sections discuss the ways in which individuals locate themselves close or far away from what they perceive as the value system associated with soap operas. I draw primarily from women's words and only selectively refer to male participants in order to demonstrate how some discourses become gender-specific.

*(1) Distance*

One of the main findings of this study is the contradiction revealed in sustained viewing of soap operas on the one hand and the dismissal of their value on the other. While most women admit watching soap operas on Arabic television, the persistence of a discourse of distance from the cultural politics these soap operas represent is striking. Women distance themselves from the dominant discourses they see reflected in the soap operas in different ways. Some are not dissimilar to the resistance to soap operas' cultural politics recorded among western audiences in earlier studies (Livingstone 1995). Others have a distinct transnational tint and relate to diasporic processes of distanciation from regional cultural politics and regional hegemonic perceptions of gender relations. I discuss different expressions of a 'sense of distance' as the tendency to locate one's subjectivity as much as possible outside the cultural and moral framework associated with Arabic language soap operas.

The subgroup that most notably distant themselves from the soap operas are middle-class younger women, though this is not an exclusively middle-class discourse. One of the reappearing discourses of distance is that of emphasizing the disconnection between watching and taking soap operas seriously.

> I watch them but they don't affect my life (Female, 18–25).

> The only reason I watch this stuff is people. People influence me (Female, 18–25).

> They [relatives] will impose soap operas upon me because it's very important part of their lives (Female, 26–45)

Locating one's self outside what is seen as a 'mass' of viewers of Arabic television is usually associated with a middle-class identity and a transnational version of media literacy. Women who position themselves in this way also demonstrate a sense of critical viewership informed by their own experience within and across different cultures. These same women often 'compare and contrast' programmes of the same genre they watch in different television networks (e.g. British and Arabic).

> I don't understand why this [fascination] is seen as only in the Arab world. It's the same with *Gossip Girl*[11]. It's not deep but people still watch it and relate to it. (Female, 18–25).

> *Eastenders*...is a perfect representation of how the English live their lives. I think they got it spot on...It is like our soaps (Female, 18–25).

These women draw from their media literacy in dissociating themselves from the soap operas and the perceived cultural context of their consumption. As media savvy audiences they also project an awareness of the banality of soap opera consumption in the context of everyday life.

A variation of this position emphasizes 'western' identity vis-à-vis migrant generation's dependence on an inevitably limited place-specific understanding of the wider world.

> My mum actually thinks it's real [stories of women being taking advantage by men in soap operas]...I suppose it's 'cause of the way they grew up back then. We live in the western world so we are exposed to this stuff anyway, whereas for them these things are new...a big shock (Female, 26–45).

This distancing mechanism reflects more than an attitude towards specific programmes; it also reflects discourses of a gendered diasporic self. It is also supported by a critical reading of gender relations in the Arab world. The historical *Bab AlHarrah* provided a reference for a number of women to express their disapproval of conservative systems of marriage in the Arab region. Some linked the serial's conservatism with the dominant framework of its consumption.

> There are a lot of Arab women who are dying to get married and I think this kind of programmes teach them what to do and what guys want (Female, 18–25).

> I kind of feel sorry for them: housewives who see these things and want to be like that (Female, 18–25).

Emphasizing their distance from female audiences in their region of origin, appears as a classist, even an Orientalist, discourse. It sometimes reveals another side of the story: a detachment from gender politics these women want to be dissociated from and which they try to resist.

> Most of the Arab families we met in London put themselves in this bubble where they think their culture is so pure... they become very protective, very extreme... their daughters wear veil from the age of 10... We've been exposed to a lot of that, especially because we are not veiled (Female, 18–25).

This example shows that for some the tensions associated with gender relations are not only located on the screen and in the Arab region but also within the local community where they live.

Women participating in most focus groups expressed some sense of distance from the Arab world and its perceived dominant value system. However, only a small minority would rigidly dissociate themselves from this system. For most, a sense of distance was ambivalent and often interchangeably used as a discourse alongside that of proximity. This ambivalence is best captured in the discussion on critical proximity in section 3.

*(2) Proximity*

The flip side of distance is proximity. With proximity I refer to participants' strong identification with their region of origin and its culture.I draw from La Pastina and Straubhaar's (2005) discussion on cultural proximity and migrant audiences. A sense of proximity was primarily revealed in two ways. First, women used soap operas as a key reference when constructing a sense of homeliness around a value system they identify as Arabic and which they recognize in televisual representations. These include family values, decency, solidarity, bravery. The second way they identify with the soap operas is expressed as genre proximity (La Pastina and Straubhaar 2005). In this case, Arabic soap operas play a comforting role in everyday life, especially through escapism, not dissimilar to other soap operas (Ang 1985; Livingstone 1991).

Alongside other media genres consumed regularly, soap operas play an important role in managing distance from people and places in the region of origin. The sense of proximity takes two generation-specific incarnations. Among older migrant women, soap operas tend to bridge geographical distance and reconcile separation. This is expressed as a nostalgic discourse, for example when older migrant women describe watching familiar places on the screen and feeling 'home-sick'. In its younger generation version, soap operas are not only supporting existing systems of communication. They also thicken and reinvent their qualities, especially when there is a sense that other people share the same products across territories.

> All my cousins watch it [*Bab AlHarrah*] in Iraq, the USA and Germany. I think everyone around the world watched *Bab AlHarrah* (Female, 18–25).

> Arabic TV feels like home cause when you watch something you can talk about it and you feel connected (Female, 18–25).

Such comments demonstrate the role of television in supporting a sense of community, perhaps not unlike a national imagined community (Anderson 1993). A community of viewers also comes together to talk about their consumption at different platforms. Pictures associated with viewing uploaded on Facebook, participation on Facebook soap opera fan groups, Skype conversations with relatives are some of the examples given in explaining how the shared cultural experiences are sustained.

> *Zahra*[12] reached such a wide demographic. My 9-year-old brother was speaking on Skype to my uncle who's 55 in Cairo and was asking him 'Did you watch *Zahra*?' (Female, 18–25).

> People put on Facebook pictures of Muhanad's house[13] (Female, 26–45).

A sense of community is supported by moral values many recognize as qualities of Arab culture. *Bab AlHarrah*, a historical serial, is often referred to as a vehicle for travelling through time and space to an ideal Arab world. While for some, as discussed in the previous section, representations of gender relations in this serial reflect an Arabic dystopia, for others *Bab AlHarrah*'s gender representations are admirable. Some of the youngest participants make comments such as: 'I like the bravery of its characters'; 'Women are so feminine and men so brave'; 'I think it's enabling communication, what is missing in any relationship'. Serials such as *Bab AlHarrah* reveal most vividly the significance of television in providing material for imagining a transnational community.

> [*Bab AlHarrah*] kind of reminds you of home. It's familiar. Circumstances are so different to our lives here. Like here, our lives are so planned. There, it's more spontaneous (Females, 18–25).

It is important to locate soap operas on Arabic television within a particularism-universalism continuum (Robertson 1993). While soap operas play a distinct role in supporting a sense of moral particularism, they are also located within a global system of television production and consumption. Earlier discussions on melodrama as a genre for female escapism (Ang 1985; Livingstone 1991) remain relevant. Only in this case, escapism takes a diasporic twist, particularly for some of the women who express their anxiety about news and events that take place in their region of origin. Soap operas represent an alternative to the news-intense televisual environment of Arabic transnational television. The words of two female participants from the 46–65 age group capture this particularity:

> Sometimes your health can't take it and you want to switch off and watch a silly soap opera.

> I watch lots of things apart from news to be honest because my nerves can't take it. Especially when something big is happening in Iraq or Palestine or Lebanon I get really stressed. So I watch soaps.

Daily media consumption of different genres becomes a way of sustaining a cognitive proximity with a region of origin (through news), while filtering it through the emotional distance offered in 'escapist' genres, such as soap operas. In this way, soap operas become supporting mechanisms of proximity, especially because they surpass tensions associated with political geographies.

*(3) Critical proximity*

For many Arab women in the diaspora, making sense of their viewing reveals an ordinary and constant shift between proximity and distance from their region of origin. Some distance themselves from the hegemonic meanings associated with soap opera production and texts, reflecting a transnational cosmopolitan habitus, while others embrace them as an element of diasporic everyday life that supports their connection with distant people and places. Cutting across proximity and distance, critical proximity demonstrates that it is possible to sustain cultural links with the region of origin without surrendering a set of values associated with their life in the diaspora. Diasporic affiliation thus becomes less of a process of choosing between either/or and more of a process combining this and thus (Beck 2006). This is particularly the case for younger participants, who tend to use a variety of media to manage relations of proximity and distance more effectively. Here, I discuss critical proximity in relation to the integrated media consumption of these participants and in relation to their reflexive engagement with mediated gender representations.

The case of the Turkish soap operas represents a fascinating case for illustrating critical proximity, especially because it has challenged the limits of gender representation. It represents a globally-recognized televisual genre of popular appeal, but it also represents a particular regional version of it: circulated and consumed in Arabic cultural spaces but not originating in the Arabic cultural space, Turkish soap operas are characterized by a cultural ambivalence which has parallels to diasporic ambivalence. As in any case of transnationally circulated soap operas, there is always an interplay between the universality of themes and the particularity of the context they are interpreted in (Liebes and Katz 1990). The thematic specificity of the Turkish soap operas has no doubt played a role in their success. Turkish soap operas are not 'other' to Arab audiences; Islam is part of the shared history of the audiences, so are arranged marriage – one of the themes in *Noor* – and family ties, especially around patriarchal figures. As the soap operas themselves play with conflicting values of tradition and modernity, and conservative religious values and secularism, they make available to diasporic audiences different layers of proximity. Women often reflected on the public debates around the Turkish soap operas and the ways in which they have challenged hegemonic models of gender relations. An exchange in one of the 18–25 groups on the main character of the soap opera *Nour* is revealing:

- Roles have been overemphasised in Arab families, you know, patriarchy. Mother is home cooking. The fact that Nour is working and leading her own life and is strong-minded makes women think: 'why am I not like this? Why can't I get someone to admire me like Muhanad[14]?

- Exactly, it raises awareness about patriarchy and female oppression.

It is important to locate this discussion at the juxtaposition of a middle-class urban Arabic experience – which has similarities to social experiences of urban middle-class women in Cairo (Abu-Lughod 2005) – and the experience of media savvy members of a western audience. Turkish soap operas usually represent an element of young women's integrated media consumption. As some say: 'I watch different television serials really'; 'Percentage-wise I used to watch more Arabic than English, but now it's the same'; 'Mostly I watch BBC and I read the news'.

In an integrated media environment where genres and formats are circulated transnationally, proximity and distance seize from being exclusively a matter of diasporic and linguistic particularity. They also become elements of gendered, generational, and classed media consumption.

> We always have this discussion. It's not just Arabic TV. Look at *90210* and the girls are over the top and extreme and everything (Female, 18–25).

> I don't watch Arabic TV. It's usually my parents (Females, 18–25).

> I watch a variety to see the different points of view and to make my own conclusions (Female, 26–45).

The more media-literate participants were, the more likely they were to locate media in the socio-political environment where they take their meanings.

> I don't think there's anything special about *Nour*... Producers look for something different and conservatives look for something to attack (Female, 18–25).

> If you watch old Arabic movies, they make *Noor* look like a nun....My grandmother could wear a mini dress and go around...now you have to wear a full veil and there's a certain decorum about how you carry yourself as a woman. *Noor* just goes full circle (Female, 18–25).

Religious conservativism was attacked by many women of different ages. For some, it merges with liberal gender conservativism in the soap operas.

> My mother is a feminist and so she says they [soap operas] are objectifying women and making fun of women (Female, 18–25).

The above represents a rare example of critique on soap operas' role in gender politics. In a variation of this discourse, some men focused on soap operas' negative effect for public debate. The words of a man in the 26–45 group capture some of these concerns:

> I was in Egypt last summer and the only thing that mattered in everyone's house was what's going on with *Muhanad*... It's funny 'cause when I was there no one had any time for politics. Whichever house you went to it was like 'How good looking is *Muhanad*' and 'Did you see that episode last night?'

In these words, this man locates himself in a position of *inside outsider* (Simmel 1908) as he feels both concerned and able to reflect from a distance on the problems with political deliberation in Egypt. His frustration about the commodification of the public sphere could also be read as frustration with the 'feminization' of the domestic and the public sphere. His comments sparked a lively debate on Turkish soaps and morality. Another participant described how an Imam in London asked men to ban these soap operas from their homes and how he was shocked with a discourse he found irrelevant to his life in London. In dismissing the conservative religious leader's inappropriate call, a third man expressed his own concerns in a way that is more compatible with western liberal values:

> You can say that these programmes have had an effect on families... I think we need to take some of the blame.

As this man dismisses the Imam's call, he appears both media literate and politically critical. At the same time, he dismisses the soap operas, reconfirming hegemonic patriarchal politics about the inferiority of a genre associated with female pleasure.

It is perhaps in genres like soap operas that some of the tensions associated with the conflicting ideologies of Arab modernity, as recorded by Kraidy and Abu-Lughod can be most vividly revealed. The space around soap opera consumption becomes a battlefield of ideas around the representation of gender, the self, and morality, in similar ways as in the case of their production (Abu-Lughod 2005). Diasporic audiences engage with the battle of ideas between the urban middle classes against Islamist 'neotraditionalization' (ibid.) and, in this way, become actively engaged with the political and cultural life in the Arab world. Yet, their exposure to these ideological struggles inevitably forces them to reflect on their own position in Arabic cultural politics. Critical proximity appears as a way, especially for younger generation, to manage ambivalence.

Critical proximity does not oppose the thesis of cultural proximity, rather it updates it in the context of the transnationalization of mediascapes. This is particularly the case with audiences who use media associated with different cultural and linguistic zones and whose engagement with most media becomes increasingly conditional and subject to a daily system of comparing and contrasting.

## Conclusions

What this discussion has demonstrated is that a popular genre, such as soap operas, can become a vehicle for imaginative travel towards the region of origin but also a vehicle for travelling back into a diasporic space. Diasporic Arab women's practices and reflections are shaped at the meeting of the soap operas' textual specificity and the realities of the social and cultural worlds they occupy: as women, as Arabs, as Muslims, but also as members of a diaspora, as Londoners, and as members of western societies. They also reflect the banality and ordinariness of media consumption, which is observed among transnational audiences as much as among other audiences (Aksoy and Robins 2000; Karanfil 2009).

Arab women in London reaffirm their sense of cultural proximity to the Middle East, but in their own gendered diasporic terms: they adopt a position of distance and relative *strangeness*, as this is defined by Simmel (1908, 1976)) to be a position of *inside outsider*. A diasporic sense of critical proximity retains some of the characteristics of the *stranger* in Simmel's sense. The stranger is a wanderer, but also represents the 'union of closeness and remoteness' (Simmel 1908(1976), p. 143). The stranger can confront all elements of a group 'objectively' because she is not bound to any particular element of it; 'an attitude that does not represent mere detachment and nonparticipation, but is a distinct structure composed of remoteness and nearness, indifference and involvement' (Simmel 1908(1976), p. 144). The interplay between remoteness and nearness captures some of the realities of diasporic attachment to cultural politics of their origin. The reaffirmation of cultural proximity *through* distance is a political position that destabilizes hegemonic understandings of *Arabness* and more specifically of female *Arabness*. It is a politics emerging in a three-dimensional space of belonging that Arab female participants construct: when they reflect on what it means to be an Arab through female practices, such as watching soap operas; when they voice desires and concerns about their life at home and in the diaspora by making comparisons and connections; when they critically reflect on the political and moral limits of an assumed singular transnational Arabic imagined community.

## Notes

1. *The research leading to these results has received funding from the European Community's Seventh Framework Programme FP7/2007–2013 under grant agreement n° 217480.*
2. I prefer the concept of 'region of origin' to 'country of origin' as the latter misses the association of diasporic groups with regions and not just nations.
3. Arabic language broadcasts take the sixth place in the world with 526 channels (Albizu 2007). The rise of satellite Arabic television emerged as a counter-point to the controlled and censored Middle Eastern national mediascapes (Kraidy 2010) but also to western media which are often seen to misrepresent Arabs and the Muslim world (Downing and Husband 2005; Gillespie 2006)

4. Television and the ideological battles it represents are of course located and linked to the broader socio-political domain where television is produced and consumed. Television audiences thus are not only audiences but also members of social groups with specific interests and experiences.
5. Telenovelas are the Latin American version of soap operas.
6. *Noor* is the name of the first very successful Turkish soap opera on Arabic television.
7. Taking the sensitivity of the issue, we did not directly ask participants about their legal status.
8. We chose the neutral 'Arab-speaker' definition in order to avoid assumptions about the participants' identities.
9. While identifying as Arabs was common among participants this was rarely the only way people would identify. Many also identified as British, Londoners, and/or members of another national community (e.g. Egyptians).
10. Popular historical soap opera produced in Syria.
11. American soap opera popular with youth.
12. Egyptian soap opera with an over-sexualised female protagonist.
13. A site reproducing *Noor*'s settings in Turkey has become a tourist attraction.
14. The main male character in the Turkish soap opera *Noor*.

# References

ABU-LUGHOD, L.ILA 2002 'Egyptian melodrama technology of the modern subject? in L. Abu-Lughod (ed.), *Remaking Women: Feminism and Modernity in the Middle East*, Princeton, NJ: Princeton University Press
—— 2005 *Dramas of Nationhood*, Chicago, IL: University of Chicago Press
—— 2010 'The marriage of feminism and Islamism in Egypt: selective repudiation as a dynamic of postcolonial cultural politics', in F.D. Ginsburg, L. Abu-Lughod and B. Larkin (eds), *Media Worlds: Anthropology on New Terrain*, Berkley, CA: University of California Press
AKSOY, ASU and KEVIN, ROBINS 2000 'Thinking across spaces: transnational television from Turkey', *in European Journal of Cultural Studies*, vol. 3, no. 3, pp. 343–65
AL-ARABIYA 2008 'Turkish Soaps Create Drama in the Arab World'. [Available from: http://www.alarabiya.net/articles/2008/10/13/58148.html [accessed 10 June 2010]]
ALBIZU, JOSU AMEZAGA 2007 'Geolinguistic regions and diasporas in the age of satellite television', *International Communication Gazette*, vol. 69, no. 3, pp. 239–61
ANDERSON, BENEDICT 1993 *Imagined Communities*, London: Verso
ANG, IEN 1985 *Watching Dallas: Soap Opera and the Melodramatic Imagination*, New York: Methuen
BARRERA, VIVIAN AND and BIELBY, D. DENISE 2001 'Places, faces, and other familiar things: the cultural experience of telenovela viewing among Latinos in the United States', *Journal of Popular Culture*, vol. 34, no. 4, pp. 1–18
BECK, ULRICH 2006 *Cosmopolitan Vision*, Cambridge: Cambridge University Press
BRINKERHOFF, JENNIFER 2009 *Digital Diasporas*, Cambridge: Cambridge University Press
BROWN, MARY ELLEN 1994 *Soap Opera and Women's Talk*, London: SAGE
BUCCIANTI, ALEXANDRA 2010 'Dubbed Turkish soap operas conquering the Arab world: social liberation or cultural alienation?', *Arab Media and Society*. [Available from: http://www.arabmediasociety.com/articles/downloads/20100330130359_Buccianti_-_for_PDF.pdf [accessed 3 March 2010]

BURCH, ELIZABETH 2002 'Media literacy, cultural proximity and TV aesthetics: why Indian soap operas work in Nepal and the Hindu diaspora', Media', *Culture and Society*, vol. 24, no. 4, pp. 571–9
COHEN, ROBIN 1997 *Global Diasporas*, London: University College London
DOWNING, JOHN AND and HUSBAND, CHARLES 2005 *Representing Race*, Thousand Oaks, CA: Sage
GEORGIOU, MYRIA 2006 *Diaspora, Identity and the Media*. Cresskill, NJ: Hampton Press
GERAGHTY, CHRISTINE 1991 *Women in Soap Operas*, Cambridge: Polity
GILLESPIE, MARIE 1995 *Television, Ethnicity and Cultural Change*, London: Routledge
—— 2006 'Transnational television audiences after September 11 2001', *Journal of Ethnic and Migration Studies*, vol. 32, no. 6, pp. 903–21
HAFEZ, KAI 2008 'Introduction', in K. Hafez (ed.), *Arab Media: Power and Weaknesses*, New York and London: Continuum
*INTERNATIONAL HERALD TRIBUNE* 2010 'Turkey's infiltration of Arab TV', in *International Herald Tribune*, 19–20 June, 2010
KARANFIL, GOKCEN 2009 'Pseudo-exiles and reluctant transnationals: disrupted nostalgia on Turkish satellite broadcasts', *MediaCulture & Society*, vol. 31, pp. 887–99
KRAIDY, MARWAN 2010 *Reality Television and Arab Politics*, Cambridge: Cambridge University Press
LA PASTINA, ANTONIO AND and STRAUBHAAR, JOSEPH 2005 'Multiple proximities between television genres and audiences: the schism between telenovelas' global distribution and local consumption', *International Communication Gazette*, vol. 67, no. 3, pp. 271–88
LEE, CHIN-CHUAN 1980 *Media Imperialism Reconsidered*, Beverly Hills, CA: Sage
LIEBES, TAMAR and ELIHU, KATZ 1990 *The Export of Meaning*, Cambridge: Polity Press
LIVINGSTONE, SONIA 1991 'Audience reception: the role of the viewer in retelling romantic drama', in James Curran and Michael Gurevitch (eds), *Mass Media and Society*, London: Hodder Arnold
—— 1995 'Making Sense of Television: The Psychology of Audience Interpretation', London: Butterworth-Heinemann
MATTELART, ARMAND, DELCOURT, XAVIER and MATTELART, MICHELLE 1984 *International Image Markets: In Search of an Alternative Perspective*, London: Comedia
MAYER, VICKI 2003 'Living telenovelas/telenovelizing life: Mexican American girls' identities and transnational telenovelas', *Journal of Communication*, vol. 53, no. 3, pp. 479–95
MILADI, NOUREDDINE 2006 'Satellite TV news and the Arab diaspora in Britain: comparing Al-Jazeera, the BBC and CNN', *Journal of Ethnic and Migration Studies*, vol. 32, no. 6, pp. 947–60
MODLESKI, TANIA 1982 *Loving with a Vengeance: Mass-Produced Fantasies for Women*, Hamden, CT: Archon
QURESHI, KAREN 2007 'Shifting promixities: news and "belonging-security"', *European Journal of Cultural Studies*, vol. 10, no. 3, pp. 294–310
RIZVI, SADAF 2006 'News cultures, security and transnational belonging: cross-generational perspectives among British Pakistani women', *European Journal of Cultural Studies*, vol. 10, no. 3, pp. 327–42
ROBERTSON, ROBERT. 1992 *Globalization: Social Theory and Global Culture*, London: Sage
SILVERSTONE, ROGER 1994 Television and Everyday Life. London and New York: Routledge

SIMMEL, GEORG 1976 'The stranger', in *The Sociology of Georg Simmel*, New York: Free Press [first published in 1908]
SINCLAIR, JOHN 1999 *Latin American Television: A Global View*, New York: Oxford
STRAUBHAAR, JOSEPH, D. 1991 'Beyond media imperialism: asymmetrical interdependence and cultural proximity', *Critical Studies in Mass Communication*, vol. 8, no. 1, pp. XX
—— 2002 '(Re)asserting national television and national identity against the global, regional and local levels of world television'. In Joseph M. Chan and McIntyre T. Bryce (eds), *In Search of Boundaries*, Westpost, CT: Ablex Publishing, pp. XX

# Online mediations in transnational spaces: cosmopolitan (re)formations of belonging and identity in the Turkish diaspora

Miyase Christensen

**Abstract**
The lives of transnational groups and individuals are marked by a spatial and imaginary split: a phenomenon wherein identity, belonging and representation have become increasingly elusive concepts, and the realm of the 'cultural' vastly important. And, the theoretical compasses of cosmopolitanism and transnationalism are particularly relevant and illuminating in considering social space, mediated communication and belonging in relation to urban diasporic communities and gendered subjectivities. The aim of this paper is to address expressions of identity and belonging at the intersection of online communicative practice and offline spatial formations, with a focus on the specificities of gendered constructions of sociality and subjectivity in the diaspora.[1]

More specifically, the paper discusses the persistence and reinvention of meanings of place as a determining factor in identity formation, especially through media use. The discussion focuses on online social media in the case of people of Turkish origin living in Stockholm. It demonstrates how these media do not necessarily detach identities from place, but rather relocate them in it. In doing so, the paper seeks to offer a more nuanced deliberation of locality vs. translocality and fixity vs. transcultural fluidity that play into individual pursuits of identity formation and of creation of cosmopolitan spaces of social belonging. The analysis and discussion is based on qualitative interviews conducted between 2008 and 2009 with Turkish migrants living in Stockholm, and is informed by secondary analysis of existing research on migrant life, media representation and residential segregation in the increasingly diverse Swedish society.

**Study frame and methodology**

As part of a larger, ongoing project exploring identity, social space and the role of mediated communication in the lives of diasporic subjects living in Sweden, this study involved semi-structured interviews with eighteen individuals (ten women and eight men) between the ages of twenty-three and forty-four, of Muslim background, secular orientation and mixed Turkish and Kurdish ethnicities. All were working during the interview period, while three female and four male participants were also studying. All of the participants use media and communication technologies (including social media) with varying degrees of competence. Five of the participants were brought to Sweden as children, six moved for professional/educational purposes in their teens and twenties, and seven were born in Sweden.

The participants lived in the suburban parts of Stockholm, such as Rinkeby, except for one woman who lived in Uppsala as a student (although she formerly lived with her parents in Rinkeby) and one man who lived in innercity Stockholm. I place particular focus on the experiences and personal accounts of the women interviewed for the purposes of this article, which explores gendered subjectivities in diasporic contexts. Most interviews were tape-recorded, unless requested otherwise. They lasted between one and two hours, and, in some cases, were accompanied with follow-up communication for clarification. The participants were recruited using the snowball technique, starting with randomly selected individuals contacted through diasporic organizations. Further recruitment was based on their personal networks. Semi-structured and open-ended interviews were conducted in order to obtain a wholesome picture of the factors that play in their perceptions and overall experiences of identity-formation and belonging, and their construction of spaces of belonging through mediated communication in their everyday lives. Interviews were conducted in Turkish and the interview questions were designed to inquire: the role of geography and social space, and place and place-making, in their lives (i.e. spatial relations in Sweden vis-à-vis home country); ethnicity, education, class and gender-related factors in relation to identity and everyday life; and, the use of everyday communication technologies for connecting and for mediating space and belonging. The study also incorporated ethnographic strategies such as site visits to and observation of residential areas populated by migrants, regular viewing of most popular online diasporic sites and attention to representations of migrants in the Swedish media.

The interviews started with questions about personal-familial background and everyday life, and were conducted in a relaxed manner to encourage dialogical discussion. All of the women and most of the men talked about their lives, world views and aspirations in relation primarily, to individual choice, cultural taste and personal lifestyles, rather than a binding sense of nationality and collective ethnic identification. During the interviews, place (i.e. the place of residence and of origin) emerged as a uniting and dividing factor, and one that is instrumental (and, can be reinvented) in establishing proximity and distance in symbolic and real terms. Women, in particular, displayed a great degree of reflexivity about the simultaneously enabling and disabling roles of ethnicity and group identity, geographic origin and everyday spatial settings and gender. As discussed below, on the whole, the study group represents a differently positioned ontological mode and experiential patterns of transnationalism than those often associated with the Turkish diaspora in Europe (see Westin 2003). Their stories and perspectives, their capacity to sustain both in-group commonality and individual difference in their identities, and the nature and boundaries of their social networks and communicative patterns are clearly constitutive of cosmopolitan life-worlds and mental geographies structured both by individual factors and the realities of the transnational migrant settings that they find themselves in.

Larsson (2006, p. 2) notes that academic studies of Muslims, both in general terms and in Sweden—and, particularly in the aftermath of 9/11—are mostly limited to religion and religiosity and they rarely study people of Muslim origin as ordinary people with secular lives. As he notes '... the Muslim community (the term is used here as a collective label for a large number of different communities) is generally described in both public and academic debates as a religious community, even though most Muslims living in Sweden are secularized' (p. 2). A supplementary aim of the article then is to go beyond commonplace perceptions of the role of religion and religiosity in the Turkish diaspora and to offer an account of (gendered) mediation and sociality in the lives of younger/fairly young Turkish migrants from a cosmopolitan frame of reference (a frame, which is not commonly associated with migrants of Muslim backgrounds). While this is an ethnographic study and does not claim representativity of the Turkish migrants in Sweden, the interviews reveal, with consistency, a high degree of reflexivity and certain patterns of mediation: strong sentiments about the close connections between space and place; and, feelings of both alienation and association with the host and home cultures that shape communicative routines and consequently borders of identity.

The paper addresses the questions raised above in three parts: the first part frames the discussion at the intersections of transnationalism, cosmopolitanism and the use of media technology in migrant contexts, and offers basic information about the history of Turkish migration in Sweden. I focus here on the tropes of migrant transnationalism and cosmopolitanism for they allow for nuanced analyses of mobility, fixity and various modes of communicative sociality. Theoretically, the scope of transnationalism provides a broad paradigmatic tool to analyse the questions of migrant identity, communication and belonging as categories embedded both in situated material and mediated realities. Cosmopolitanism as a framework to locate both rooted and world-oriented dispositions can certainly be extended to understand identity and positionality in certain transnational settings and online social constellations originating therein. Yet, transnationality or transborder mobility alone are by no means readily equitable to cosmopolitanism, and transnationalism and cosmopolitanism cannot be conflated. In this study, cosmopolitanism is employed as an analytical tool in discussing certain positionalities and ethical/cultural orientations of the participants who live in a transnational social context.

The second part of the paper empirically locates intersectionality between online space, offline locality/territoriality, communicative sociality and gender. For participants, material realities are primarily located in the urban spatial context while their mediated ones are shaped through complex systems of networked sociality. This part draws from data revealing the persistence and significance of place and territoriality and reflects on the primacy of *the city* over *the nation*.

The final part takes issue with the notions of mobility, agency and expressivity (in relation to the ways in which these notions are embodied in the communication process), and the positioning of gendered, cosmopolitan subjectivity in participants' lives. Drawing from Hetherington (1998), expressivity is taken to involve, not only rational choices and direct deliberative action, but also emotions and sense of belonging that materialize in daily life through spatial–both material and virtual–practice.

## Transnational migrant settings, mediated communication and the question of cosmopolitanism

With the increase observed in the rate of global material, human and virtual flows, both transnational-translocal relationships and everyday situated experiences and deterritorialized and reterritorialized dimensions (Smith 2001) have become part and parcel of the ways in which migrants construct their identities (cf. Glick-Schiller, Basch and Blanc 1995; Vertovec 2001) cutting across fixed notions of belonging (Dwyer

2000). Theoretical constructions of transnationalism as social morphology, type of consciousness, mode of cultural reproduction and reconstruction of place and locality (Vertovec 1999) are relevant and significant in this study. Transnational urbanism (Smith 2001), which further accentuates the significance of physical location and communicative practice in the face of pervasive processes of denationalization (Sassen 2008) adds more nuance to our understanding of networked sociality and mediations of social space in diasporic contexts.

In this study, transnationalism provides a broad contextual framework and an epistemological plane on which to locate emergent dynamics (e.g. shifts in power geometries) and social phenomena (e.g. cosmopolitan*ization*) arising from the increasingly complex forms and practices of actual and virtual mobility, fixity, mediation and belonging vis-à-vis everyday diasporic realities. As noted in recent literature (see Vertovec 2009; Held 2010), there has been a return to cosmopolitanism both in cultural studies and political science to account for a variety of developments and phenomena from multiculturalism and marginal communities to global social movements and environmental crises. Although the Kantian, Enlightenment origins of cosmopolitan theory are often associated with rootlessness and abstraction from particular local and cultural belonging (e.g. Hannerz 1990), certain other streams in the theorization of cosmopolitanism have been particularly instrumental in counterbalancing the elitism and top-downism commonly associated with the concept.

As Werbner (2008) notes, the theory of cosmopolitanism from the 1990s onwards has striven to go beyond interpretations of cosmopolitanism as only universal, open and, above all, 'Western', and to include local, rooted and historically and spatially situated dimensions that can be accommodated by the ethical horizon of cosmopolitanism. Werbner's (ibid) linking together universal enlightenment and local specificity through the discursive frame of 'vernacular cosmopolitanism' resonates well with the ways in which the study participants position themselves on a plane of contradictory opposites: local, cultural, rooted proximities and loyalties and an ability and eagerness to maintain a transnational, open, modernist and individualist ethical outlook. Robbins' (1998) 'actually existing cosmopolitanisms'; Clifford's (1998) ideologically progressive 'discrepant cosmopolitanisms'; Stevenson's (2002) efforts to think multiculturalism, cultural citizenship and cosmopolitanism together and connecting such thinking to questions of 'identity formation *within* and *between* national societies' (emphasis added) are all exemplary of the conceptual apparatus that frame the study presented here in meaningful ways. Clifford's (1998, p. 362) note of cosmopolitanism as encountered by people in 'worldly, productive sites of crossing,' is particularly useful in understanding the role of urban space and 'connexity' of both difference and diversity and universality. His 'discrepant cosmopolitanisms' is invoked here in referring to a process of continuous rectification of our perceptions of social distance and moral/cultural borders.

The understanding that guides this particular study is one that conceives cosmopolitanism in relation to mediations of (re)attachment (e.g. to place) and positionality based on location and culture as well as to detachment and openness. Further useful here is Glick-Schiller, Darieva and Gruner-Domic's (2011) conceptualization of cosmopolitanism as 'simultaneous rootedness and openness to shared human emotions, experiences and aspirations' (2011, p. 399). Attachment and positionality in diaspora, however, are far from being singular, and always multiple, contested, and, at times, pragmatically constituted.

This multiplicity is quite pronounced in the case of the Turkish migrants living in Sweden. Turkish labour influx to Sweden, mostly from rural Turkey and mostly from the town of Kulu, started in the mid-1960s and continued until the first half of the 1970s. From the 1980s onwards most migrants originating from Turkey were Kurds seeking refuge on the grounds of political persecution, or, to a lesser extent, those migrating for family reunion (Westin 2003). Today, there are around 65,000 residents of Turkish origin in Sweden (of various Turkish and Kurdish ethnicities), most residing in the suburban areas such as Rinkeby of Stockholm, making them the tenth largest ethnic minority group in Sweden. Slightly more than half of the members of this community were born in Turkey, and the remaining are second and third generation members born in Sweden (Westin 2003). Transnationalism and transnational ties are embodied, to varying degrees, in the sense of maintaining continuous contact with those left behind in Turkey, amongst themselves as migrants living in Stockholm and with others (Turkish or otherwise) living elsewhere. As included in the sample group of this study, there are also individuals and families who came and settled in Stockholm for professional and educational purposes. As revealed through the interviews, there is as much difference as there is commonality within the Turkish diasporic community in Sweden.

Amongst the participants, there is a high level of consciousness about questions of inter/intra-group positionalities and identities. It is precisely these tension fields arising out of such multiplicities, and, realities and aspirations that simultaneously feed from and turn against each other, that give way to a cosmopolitan state of orientation. Caglar (2002), in referring to Clifford (1998), suggests we should consider cosmopolitanism as a 'reality of (re)attachments with multiple affiliations.... Cosmopolitanism can still be conceived of as a mode of attachment, which, by entailing multiple, uneven and non-exclusive affiliations challenges the conventional notions of locality as well as of belonging,' (Caglar 2002, p. 180). As she surmises, what determines cosmopolitan formations and mental orientations is not the existence or absence of attachments but the ways in which such attachments are enacted and how individuals navigate their lives across multiple domains of choice and (in)formally conceived reciprocal, unilateral and forced obligations and allegiances (e.g. familial and traditional boundaries).

In line with these analyses of cosmopolitanism, the present study is illustrative of expressions of cosmopolitanism that do not necessarily manifest themselves as a commitment to achieving a western cosmopolitan ideal (see also Tarrow [2005] on cognitive vs. relational cosmopolitanism). The ways in which individuals and groups relate to the global and the local, the self and the *Other* (including their own *Others*), and the distant and the near are far more complex than what could simply be grasped under categories such as 'rootedness and fixity' vs. 'mobility and flexibility'. The interview data point to a complex variety of elements that underlie these individuals' migrant existence and mind frame such as a sharp understanding of the current global and national conjuncture; an awareness and willingness to accept and negotiate the 'relativity of one's own social position and culture' (Beck 2004, p. 131); and an equally sharp awareness of the different positionalities and *Others-within*.

As research shows, Information and Communication Technologies (ICTs) and diasporic media play an increasingly significant role in fostering emerging identities or sustaining identities (cf. Georgiou 2006; Bailey, Georgiou and Harindranath 2007). There is a rich body of literature exploring the linkages between digital communication use and migrant communities (cf. Nakamura 2002; Adams and Ghose 2003, to name but a few) in relation to both the place of mediation in the everyday lives of migrants and in relation to political deliberation and cultural expression. Alonso and Oiarzabal (2010) point to the significance of applications that enable 'produsage' and to the ways in which the majority of internet content will come from users themselves, with migrants in particular contributing to this significantly through social networks.

Yet, deterritorializing tendencies of global forces (Sassen 2008) in various spheres of life notwithstanding, place and power geometries (Massey 1993) embedded therein retain their significance with offline power often migrating to online spaces. Mobility runs parallel to significant and complex forms of territorial anchoredness (spatially, culturally and institutionally) in the lives of transnational migrants and such fixity is also challenged through mediations of place and spatial relations. This calls into question earlier conceptualizations of online space as 'placeless space' (Christensen, Jansson and Christensen, 2011). Further, increasing numbers of studies have pointed to the need to introduce a 'place lens' (Gielis 2009) and to emphasize the importance of 'the city', 'migrant congregations of urban settlements' and 'translocalities' (cf. Sinatti 2006) in the study of migrant transnationalism and cosmopolitan communication practices. Harvey's (1989) conceptualization of spatiality and temporality in which mobility and fixity are equally generative forces and Massey's (1994) point about the stratifying role of gender (amongst other factors) in the (re)location of subjectivities through both fixity and mobility are of significance here. Thus, examining the juxtaposition of the spatial flexibility of the online and the significance of place and locale is a necessary starting point in order to capture the connection between the transnational diasporic condition, communicative sociality and cosmopolitan (re)formations.

### Where the material meets the virtual: the case of the Turkish migrants in Stockholm

To start with, the city of residence and the city of origin have significant material and symbolic bearings that impact upon patterns of sociality, communication and belonging. Apart from the role of social determinants, such as class, education and gender and of individual preferences, two elements reign supreme in shaping social relations in the diaspora: spatial configurations of the city itself and the persistence of territorial extensions (both translocally and transnationally). The domain of the city as a site which embodies immediacy and various forms of material exclusion and inclusion play a far greater role in the social imaginaries of the migrant subjects than the more ephemeral, symbolic realm of the national. In the city, certain sites and places have 'social centrality' (Hetherington 1998) and take on a symbolic role. Shopping centres, common meeting points, cultural centres, neighbourhoods and various other forms of nodes constitute such common places. Of importance in this study are the relative sensory textures of the suburban migrant areas and of the centre as experienced by the participants. The migrants' sense of belonging is closely linked with their physical presence in the city as they are positioned 'in between' the peripheral and the central spaces of identity. One particular point that comes out of the interview data is the participants' articulations of strong attachment to Stockholm and a heightened sense of reflexivity (and ethical openness) they possess, not least due to their experiencing both the migrant-suburban and the central realms of the city. In relation to its constitutive power for forming and performing identities, the experiential realm of the city and the way it mediates between tradition and liberation then could be seen in juxtaposition to the more symbolic and abstract realm of *the national* (and its politics and institutional culture).

In the particular case of Sweden, there is a disjuncture between the national imaginary, which celebrates the nation as one of the world pioneers in foreign aid, social and gender equality and a very high per capita refugee intake rate on the one hand and the spatial configuration of its urban areas on the other. As Pred observes (1997):

> Many of the first and second generation immigrants and refugees racialized by the majority population have developed forms of collective identity and cultural reworking that cannot be separated from the ways in which they have been spatially segregated in the Stockholm, Göteborg and Malmö metropolitan areas (pp. 395–6).

Stockholm is marked by spatial segregation and the subsidized 'Million Homes' areas in the outskirts of the city such as Rinkeby, built in the 1960s and 1970s by the Social Democrats to solve the housing problem, are inhabited mostly by migrants today. Consequently, these areas have become homogenously and stereotypically *alien* and *immigrant* (see Pred 1997; Christensen, C. 2008). As Andersson (2007) details, the Turkish-born population is fairly concentrated in large housing estates built as part of the Million Homes Programme. On the whole, reductionist accounts, particularly in relation to Muslims, play a significant role in the national social imaginary as recent studies suggest. Hvitfelt (2002) notes that television news associate Muslims and Islam primarily with violence and war; and, Westin (2003) observes that Turkish people are seen as ethnically distant with strong cultural attachments by the Swedish society.

The majority of the participants interviewed for this study indicated that they feel, in certain social instances, a strong alienation from the society, as a result of popular perceptions about their origin, appearance and cultural backgrounds. A number of the female participants said that they felt native Swedes displayed prejudice (or in some cases mere naïveté) against females of certain ethnic origin. One university student remarked:

> I can see it in their [native Swedes'] eyes that when they look at me they think 'oh, another one of those *svartskalle*'[2]. And, they get shocked when they hear my native Swedish accent. I am Turkish, educated and non-veiled. They don't know what to make of me (Female in her twenties).

As this and a number of the other participants noted, such instances of feeling *Other*ed both within the diasporic community and by the larger society leads to a search for alternative means of sociality, particularly using online platforms, which in the case of one participant went as far as starting a Facebook group for 'equally open-minded individuals' (personal interview 2008). On the one hand, there is a general, encompassing element of commonality of identity and identification with a shared historicity, language and everyday culture within the Turkish diasporic community in Sweden. On the other hand, there is a great deal of diversity, and pronounced elements of generational, gender and class differences, and antagonisms arising from both territorial and class origins of certain sub-groups.[3] Strong feelings of antagonism and alienation were noted particularly in relation to certain subgroups of Turkish migrants' discriminatory and *Other*ing attitudes toward other individuals and groups of Turkish origin. While its findings cannot be generalized, the study clearly indicates that identity, belonging and representation are far from unitary but very much contested and play a significant role in patterns of communication and mediated socialization amongst the Turkish migrants of Stockholm. Migrants' physical location in the city and the degree to which they interact with the larger society are linked with their mediation habits and the virtual channels they prioritize for everyday socialization.

During the interviews, it was pointed out that the older members of the diaspora appear to have closer in-group ties and they consume traditional Turkish media (mostly television), while the younger members are in touch with the Swedish society to a larger extent and have different media consumption habits. One participant, a woman in her twenties, pointed out that she only watches Turkish television when she visits her parents. As was revealed by a number of the participants, some of the older/first generation members of the diaspora are connecting through translocal sites (or 'village sites' as the participant referred to them) displaying communicative habits that can be seen as the extensions of their sense of spatial belonging. The village sites are online domains launched to represent certain locales (villages or towns) in Turkey and their people living in Turkey *and* across the globe. As such, they are both transnational and geographically defined. http://www.kululuyuz.biz/ and www.serefli.org were brought up as popular examples frequented by Turkish migrants in Sweden and elsewhere. For the older generation (noted as casual observations by the participants in relation to their families/relatives), everyday sociality appears to take shape through face-to-face interaction with other migrants of Turkish origin while the participants' own social connections are more multi-nodal and mediated in character bringing together elements of physical locale and virtuality in complex ways.

Study participants also pointed to the existence of fields of strong tension between those who have been power-holders and gatekeepers in representing the diasporic community over extended periods of time and those who lead or belong to newer, alternative social formations (e.g. associations or online portals). Online social media were consistently pointed to as platforms where communication assumes a more expressive form. This links to forms of belonging as sought outside the bounds of more commonplace versions of diasporic, ethnic and sub-group identity, and where 'the cultural' and 'the political' are intertwined leading to the rise of cosmopolitan sensibilities and new communities of choice and communal belonging. Likewise, Werbner, R. (2008), cited in Werbner, P. 2008) argues that public cosmopolitanism is *de facto* a socially inclusive political project that takes the form of linking like-minded individuals and groups. This project involves, as he notes, 'first, the restless quest for the further horizon; second, the imperative of moral re-centring; and third, the constructing and transcending of difference,' (p.15). The significance of mediated sociality and online media here is that such platforms do not only serve as communication media but precisely as spaces for moral re-centring and for re-shaping the form, scale and context of everyday relational experiences toward more cosmopolitan horizons.

Online networked sociality, in particular, provides a spatial matrix to forge, sustain, resist and appropriate diverse modes of representation. Sites such as Facebook are used as meeting places by both existing groups and communities, and as breeding grounds for new social constellations: 'Isvecli Turkler (Swedish Turks)'; 'Isvec Turkleri (Turks of Sweden)'; 'Turkar i Stockholm (Turks in Stockholm)'; 'Isvec'te Yasayan Turkler (Turks living in Sweden)'; 'Isvec'teyiz (We are in Sweden)', moderated by the offline Sweden 'Idea and Culture Association'; and, 'A Group for the Swedish Turkish' constituted some of the popular Facebook groups during the research process in 2008–9. In addition, some offline institutions also have their own Facebook groups. The Facebook groups listed above all bear spatial associations through which the *centre* is reclaimed by its marginalized members. Appiah's (1998) discussion of rooted cosmopolitanism and of how cosmopolitans start from membership in morally and emotionally significant collectivities such as ethnic communities and families is meaningful here in understanding the role of significations of place. While national space (Turkey, Sweden) and urban space (Stockholm) are precisely the containers of ethnic, cultural, geographic divisions, of segregation and ethnically-produced residential concentration (i.e. 'migrant neighbourhoods'), imagined and mediated reinventions of place, such as the Facebook groups, that embrace difference as much as similarity, serve the purpose of a cosmopolitan recentring and spatially-enacted ethical recalibration. As such, place remains very much part of identity negotiation and virtual sociality in transnational settings.

## Thinking mobility, agency and gender together

As argued, material conditions, concrete boundaries and restrictions/scarcities on the one hand and mediated transgressions on the other, factor heavily in shaping agency and positionality amongst Turkish migrants. Reinventions/reclaiming of place as a cosmopolitan discursive tactic and strategic practice to generate 'open' spaces of diversity is routinely challenged by spatial proximity and fixity which harbours gendered delimitations of choice and agency on an everyday basis. In her discussion of social stratification, Anthias (2001) critiques the view that regards gender and ethnicity as social constructions that are commonly associated with the symbolic or cultural realms, while class is seen as relating to material inequality. She suggests a formulation in which claims and struggles over various types of resources take place in terms of gender, ethnicity/race and class. In the case of transnational migrant communities, class and ethnicity are often conflated and ethnicity is often perceived as a marker for class and educational level by the larger society. In the case of Muslim groups, perceptions of gender (often seen as a mere product of ethnicity and religiosity) are further complicated.

Gender dynamics within and outside of the transnational group are generative of stratification, and of various forms of spatialities and positionalities. Here, consideration of mobility–in its broadest sense–and reflexivity as dual forces navigating agentic disposition and expressivity offers an analytical gateway to approaching gendered cosmopolitan subjectivities. Hannam, Sheller and Urry (2006, p. 4) make note of 'the power and politics of discourses and practices of mobility in creating both movement and stasis,' and Fay (2007, p. 1) suggests that 'women have come to participate in voluntary movement in more agentic ways than possibly ever before.' Such a perspective helps us to better grasp the gendered reverberations of confrontations over power and identity, which result in instances of both persistence of traditional social constructions and annihilation/bypassing of them.

While younger women in the Turkish diaspora have a relatively high degree of social visibility in educational, professional and public life, they are far from untouched by social pressure and monitoring within the diasporic community and by discriminatory treatment in the larger social field as it was noted during the interviews. The segregated nature of urban areas and the tension fields between the migrant groups and the larger society have significant consequences for women. An affluent young female who holds a high level position in one of the diasporic representative institutions remarked:

> It is difficult to pursue an independent lifestyle here if you are a woman. You know... You start dating someone and somebody's

mother sees you at a café and tells your mom. This kind of thing. There is a lot of close monitoring (Female in her twenties).

A similar observation was noted by a young male in relation to his larger family and their concern over 'cultural corruption': 'My aunt and uncle keep a very close eye on my two [female] cousins.... The girls use the internet heavily though and it's difficult for my aunt and uncle to control that,' (Male in his twenties).

As the interviews illustrate, in addition to reinforcing existing and engendering new spaces of belonging, online groups also allow for enactments of *phantasmic belonging*: a seamless form of interaction for individuals (in this case women) who do not necessarily wish to subscribe to identificatory categories by way of becoming members but want to partake both for ontological security and simple sociality. As discussed earlier, transnational communities, particularly Muslim ones, have been more prone to essentializing attitudes, particularly after 9/11. Hence, current practices of identity formation/assertion, communicative action and certain cultural reflexes toward both protectionism and rejection of certain labels need to be seen in that context. As one participant remarked:

I only use Facebook to get in touch with people that I am away from. I don't use it for its group function.... Also, I don't want to join those groups because it [the identity they represent] is not important for me. Turkish, Kurdish, Assyrian, Armenian... I don't want to take on an identity like that (Female in her twenties).

A male participant in his twenties commented on how he uses his Facebook account to form different groupings. He posts his photos and other personal information in creative ways so that he can be discreet about his sexual identity in family circles and diasporic networks, while revealing his choice openly to other contacts. Various other forms of online social activity and ways to avoid building concrete and visible ties were brought up during the interviews. As such, online social media platforms, such as Facebook, not only facilitate ordinary networking of individuals and groups, but also pursue regimes of *in*visibility and concealment, particularly by younger individuals and females who incorporate various communicative tactics to avoid power geometries and social monitoring. By incorporating a *mobile agency,* the individuals interviewed for this study both sustain their gender roles within the community and enter into new playing fields through mediation which is not easily penetrable by in-group control apparatuses. The mobility (of agency) in question eases crossing of social borders, particularly when and where cosmopolitan openness is challenged by parochial protectionism and intervention.

Consequently, a disposition toward appropriating simultaneously local/particularistic and savvy/universalistic sensibilities, and accompanying tactics to carve out publicly intimate spaces is revealed at the juncture of offline social space and mediated communication. These intersectional communicative spaces engender a specific experience of belonging, empathy and (dis)trust 'which does without the consolation of idealized images of community and communication' (Silverstone 1999, cited in Barnett 2004, p. 66).

To go back to the question of cosmopolitanism, Tomlinson (1999, p. 195) draws from Hannerz's (1990) typology of cosmopolitans and locals, in suggesting that the cosmopolitan is not the ideal type to be opposed to the local.

> She [sic] is precisely someone who is able to live—ethically, culturally—*in both the global and the local at the same time.* Cosmopolitans can recognize their own cultural dispositions and negotiate as equals with other autonomous locals (emphasis in original).

A heightened sense of reflexivity, as Tomlinson is alluding to here, accompanies mobile agency and tactful subjectivity, qualities which seem to correspond to the discourse developed by diasporic women participating in the current study.

It is worth noting that reflexivity is one concept that has been highly valorized in the globalization, cosmopolitanism and mobilities discourses alike (and, at times, to the point of downplaying the role of material exclusions and overbearing structures). While the role of social structures and resources remains very much vital, reflexivity takes various shapes. In many instances, reflexivity manifests itself as a self-regulated expressive capacity not necessarily engendering instant social change by radically shifting the power geometry but nonetheless enabling individuals to live–ethically, culturally–in an in-betweenness by continuously forming and adapting comfort zones around attaching locality and disembedding universalism. Such a tendency is clearly a common characteristic shared by the female participants in this study. Urry's mobilities (both symbolic and real), particularly in relation to the individuals and groups involved within this study, also remain instrumental as (1) movement between identificatory categories and social domains is occurring incessantly and in complex ways; and (2) some groups and individuals (such as the women in this study) incorporate a heightened sense of self-awareness and a more organic form of reflexivity that is routinized (even if it is not immediately privileging in material terms) rather than occasional (cf. Christensen, 2011). One participant noted that she follows Turkish TV programmes in order not to lose her social presence in certain settings.

Such forms of tactfulness that are developed in transnational settings have precisely to do with the fact that self-realization between obligations, restrictions and aspirations necessitates an ability to continuously observe situations, make informed choices and keep a fine balance between different positionalities.

## In conclusion: life on the brink of flux and continuity

Mediated communication is far from offering imminently and radically transformative experiences and privileges lacking in the offline domain. While contemporary forms of mediation can yield ruptures–of varying scale and form–in the experience of territoriality and belonging, and in the norms that govern the multiple spheres of life, continuities prevail and must be accounted for. It is precisely in such contexts that vernacular, discrepant forms of cosmopolitanism find venues of expression in search of new ethical vistas and new relational experiences. Diasporas are heterogeneous and it is often the case that segregating and *Other*ing practices in the host country combined with ethnic and spatial isolation yield nationalistic, even militant, reflexes of protectionism, not cosmopolitanism. Turkish diaspora is no different, yet the results of this study are illustrative of two significant, dialectically constituted, trends.

Firstly, although mediated activity epitomizes a significant portion of everyday diasporic life, spatially-defined limitations (such as segregated neighbourhoods) and place-bound belonging (to the cities of origin and of current residence) determine, to a great degree, both material possibilities and relational and symbolic boundaries. Gender adds another dimension to how individuals are positioned vis-à-vis mobility and fixity (Massey 1994). Secondly, constraint and fixity rooted in both demographic and spatial factors are dynamically challenged from within. In the current case, this takes the form of subverting and symbolically reinventing the very containers of 'closure', such as place and by generating altered spaces of belonging open to new relational experiences. Online spaces of connecting accommodates diverse forms of togetherness and voice and extended possibilities to see the world from a variety of *Others*' perspectives. While it is certainly not the case that Turkish diaspora–or any diaspora–in its entirety, can be studied from the analytical stance of cosmopolitanism, a thickly textured world-orientedness and a true and conscious openness are highly visible features amongst certain transnational groups and individuals.

Women, such as those who participated in this study, juggle between individual choice and aspirations and traditionalism and rootedness. Their communicative practices and the solutions they seek, without effacing cultural and individual differences, are clearly cosmopolitan.

In sum, while transnationalism and cosmopolitanism are often invoked in discursive frames of deterritorialization and placelessness, persistence of elements of spatial fixity and (trans)locality need to be seen as part of lived transnationality and global mobility. Understanding identity, communication and belonging in diasporic frames of existence requires unbundling, through situated research, of the ways in which mediation, gendered agency, spatial/territorial materiality and belonging feed into and from each other.

## Notes

1. Akin to Axel (2004), I take diaspora to mean a globally mobile category of identification rather than a community of individuals dispersed from a homeland; and, as constituted through a complex web of everyday social practices rather than displacement.
2. Svartskalle is a derogatory Swedish word, similar to nigger in effect, literally meaning black skull in reference to the darker hair color of certain immigrant groups.
3. Turkish migrants form neighbourhoods based on where they come from in Turkey

## References

ADAMS, PAUL C. and GHOSE, RINA 2003 'India.com: the construction of a space between', *Progress in Human Geography*, vol. 4, no. 27, pp. 417–37
ALONSO, ANDONI and OIRZIBAL, PEDRO J. (eds) 2010 *Diasporas in the New Media Age: Identity, Politics, and Community*, Reno, NV: University of Nevada Press
ANDERSSON, ROGER 2007 "Ethnic residential segregation and integration processes in Sweden", in Karen Schönwälder (ed.), *Residential Segregation and the Integration of Immigrants: Britain, the Netherlands and Sweden, Discussion Paper*, Berlin: Social Science Research Center, pp. 61–90
ANTHIAS, FLOYA 2001 'The material and the symbolic in theorizing social stratification: issues of gender, ethnicity and class', *British Journal of Sociology*, vol. 52, no. 3, pp. 367–90
APPIAH, KWAME ANTHONY 1998 'Cosmopolitan patriots', in Cheah Pheng and Robbins Bruce (eds), *Cosmopolitics: Thinking and Feeling Beyond the Nation*, Minneapolis, MN: University of Minnesota Press, pp. 91–116
AXEL, BRIAN K. 2004 'The context of diaspora', *Cultural Anthropology*, vol. 19, no. 1, pp. 26–60
BAILEY, OLGA, GEORGIOU, MYRIA and HARINDRANATH, RAMASWAMI (eds) 2007 *Transnational Lives and the Media: Re-Imagining Diaspora*, London: Palgrave
BARNETT, CLIVE 2004 'Neither poison nor cure: space, scale and public life in media theory', in Couldry Nick and McCarthy Anna (eds), *Mediaspace: Place, Scale and Culture in a Media Age*, London: Routledge, pp. 58–74
BECK, ULRICH 2004 'Cosmopolitical realism: on the distinction between cosmopolitanism in philosophy and the social sciences', *Global Networks*, vol. 4, no. 2, pp. 131–56
CAGLAR, AYSE 2002 'Media corporatism and cosmopolitanism', in Vertovec Steven and Cohen Robin (eds), *Conceiving Cosmopolitanism: Theory, Context and Practice*, Oxford: Oxford University Press, pp. 180–90
CHRISTENSEN, CHRISTIAN 2008 'Defending, representing or branding? gringo magazine and Swedish multiculturalism', in Christensen Miyase and Erdogan Nezih (eds), *Shifting Landscapes: Film and Media in European Context*, Newcastle: Cambridge Scholars Publishing, pp. 221–40

CHRISTENSEN, MIYASE 2011 'Online Social Media, Communicative Practice and Complicit Surveillance in Transnational Contexts', in Christensen Miyase, Jansson Andre and Christensen Christian (eds), *Online Territories: Globalization, Mediated Practice and Social Space*, New York: Peter Lang, pp. 222–38.
CHRISTENSEN, MIYASE, JANSSON, ANDRE and CHRISTENSEN, CHRISTIAN 2011 'Globalizaion, mediated practice and social space: assessing the means and metaphysics of online territories', in Christensen Miyase, Jansson Andre and Christensen Christian (eds), *Online Territories: Globalization, Mediated Practice and Social Space*, New York: Peter Lang, pp. 1–11
CLIFFORD, JAMES 1998 'Mixed feelings', in Cheah Pheng and Robbins Bruce (eds), *Cosmopolitics: Thinking and Feeling Beyond the Nation*, Minneapolis, MN: University of Minnesota, pp. 362–71
DWYER, C.LAIRE 2000 'Negotiating diasporic identities: young British south Asian Muslim women', *Womens Studies International Forum*, vol. 23, no. 4, pp. 475–86
FAY, MICHAELA 2007 'Mobile subjects, mobile methods: doing virtual ethnography in a feminist online network', *Forum: Qualitative Social Research*, vol. 8, no. 3, Art. 14
GEORGIOU, MYRIA 2006 'Diaspora, Identity and the Media' , Diasporic Transnationalism and Mediated Spatialities, New York: Hampton Press
GIELIS, RUBEN 2009 'A global sense of migrant places: towards a place perspective in the study of migrant transnationalism', *Global Networks*, vol. 9, no. 2, pp. 271–87
GLICK-SCHILLER, NINA, BASCH, LINDA and BLANC, CRISTINA 1995 'From immigrant to transmigrant: theorizing transnational migration', *Anthropological Quarterly*, vol. 68, no. 1, pp. 48–63
GLICK-SCHILLER, NINA, TSYPYLMA, DARIEVA and GRUNER-DOMIC, SANDRA 2011 'Defining cosmopolitan sociability in a transnational age. An introduction', *Ethnic and Racial Studies*, vol. 34 no. 3, pp. 399–418
HANNAM, KEVIN, SHELLER, MIMI and URRY, JOHN 2006 'Mobilities, immobilities and moorings', *Mobilities*, vol. 1, no. 1, pp. 1–22
HANNERZ, ULF 1990 'Cosmopolitans and locals in world culture', in Featherstone Mike (ed.), *Global Culture: Nationalism, Globalization and Modernity*, London: Sage, pp. 237–51
HARVEY, DAVID 1989 *The Condition of Postmodernity*, Oxford: Blackwell
HELD, DAVID 2010 *Cosmopolitanism: Ideals, Realities and Deficits*, Cambridge: Polity Press
HETHERINGTON, 1998 *Expressions of Identity: Space, Performance, Politics*, London: Sage
HVITFELT, HÅKAN 2002 'A New Media World', in Hvitfelt Håkan and Nygre Gunnar (eds), *Toward the Media-world 2020: Journalism, Technology and the Market*, Sweden: Studentlitteratur, pp. 53–5
LARSSON, GÖRAN 2006 'Islam and Muslims in the Swedish media and academic research: with a bibliography of English and French literature on Islam and Muslims in Sweden, EU Working Papers, RSCAS No. 2006/36, European University Institute. Available at: http://cadmus.eui.eu/handle/1814/6318?show=full [Accessed 15 January 2009]
MASSEY, DOREEN 1993 'Power-geometry and a progressive sense of place', in John Bird, Barry Curtis, Tim Putnam, Robertson George and Tickner Lisa (eds), *Mapping the Futures: Local Cultures, Global Change*, London: Routledge, pp. 59–69
—— 1994 *Space, Place and Gender*, Cambridge: Polity
NAKAMURA, LISA 2002 *Cybertypes: Race, Ethnicity and Identity on the Internet*, New York: Routledge
PRED, A.LLAN 1997 'Somebody else, somewhere else: racisms, racialized spaces and the popular geographical imagination in Sweden', *Antipode*, vol. 29, no. 4, pp. 383–416
ROBBINS, BRUCE 1998 'Actually existing cosmopolitanism. cosmopolitics –thinking and feeling beyond the nation', in Pheng Cheah and Bruce Robbins (eds) *Cosmopolitics: Thinking and Feeling Beyond the Nation*, Minneapolis, MN: University of Minnesota Press, pp. XX–XX

SASSEN, SASKIA 2008 *Territory, authority and rights: from medieval to global assemblages*, Princeton, NJ: Princeton University Press
SINATTI, G.IULIA 2006 'Diasporic cosmopolitanism and conservative translocalism: narratives of nation among Senegalese migrants in Italy', *Studies in Ethnicity and Nationalism*, vol. 6, no. 3, pp. 30–50
SMITH, M.ICHAEL PETER 2001 *Transnational Urbanism: Locating Globalization*, Oxford: Blackwell
TAROOW, SIDNEY 2005 *The New Transnational Activism*, Cambridge: Cambridge University Press
TOMLINSON, JOHN 1999 *Globalization and Culture*, Cambridge: Polity Press
VERTOVEC, S.TEVEN 1999 'Conceiving and researching transnationalism', *Ethnic and Racial Studies*, vol. 22, no. 2, pp. 447–62
—— 2001 "Transnationalism and identity", *Journal of Ethnic and Migration Studies*, vol. 27, no. 4, pp. 573–82
—— 2009 *Transnationalism*, London: Routledge
WERBNER, PNINA 2008 'Introduction: towards a new cosmopolitan anthropology', in Pnina Werbner (ed.), *Anthropology and the New Cosmopolitanism: Rooted, Feminist and Vernacular Perspectives*, Oxford: Berg Publisher, pp. 1–32
WESTIN, C.HARLES 2003 'Young people of migrant origin in Sweden', *International Migration Review*, vol. 37, no. 4, pp. 987–1010

# Migrant African women: tales of agency and belonging

Olga Guedes Bailey

**Abstract**

This paper explores issues of belonging and agency among asylum seekers and refugee women of African origin in the UK. It discusses the ways these women engendered resistance in their everyday life to destitution, lack of cultural recognition, and gender inequality through the foundation of their own non-governmental organization, African Women's Empowerment Forum, AWEF, a collective 'home' space.

The focus of this account is on migrant women's agency and self-determination for the exercise of choice to be active actors in society. It points to what might be an important phenomenon on how local grassroots movements are challenging the invisibility of asylum seekers' and refugees' lives and expanding the notion of politics to embrace a wider notion of community politics with solidarity.

AWEF is the embodiment of a social space that resonates the 'in-between' experience of migrant life providing stability to the women members regarding political and community identification.

**Introduction**

Europe is a changing place marked predominantly by neo-liberal market ideologies and conservative politics. This place is characterized by an imagined homogeneous historiography of nationhood, which is compromised by the existence of cultural diversity and otherness (Comaroff and Comaroff 2009). As the political claims of minority groups on redistribution and cultural recognition intensifies, European nation-states have had to come to terms with difference and, in many instances, have granted a variety of measures to counter social and political marginalization (Song 2007). But this does not mean that institutional practices and everyday social relations have changed. For example, while there has been an increase in levels of participation of multiethnic groups in British society, and a more positive approach to difference and diversity in official policy on race, ethnicity and culture, there has also been an increase of less tolerant public discourses and migration policies, especially regarding asylum seekers (Bailey and Harindranath 2006).

In this context, multicultural groups, including asylum seekers and refugee women, are becoming important actors in the struggle for economic redistribution and cultural and political recognition. Fraser (2008) argues that as cultural injustices are entangled and support those of a socio-economic nature, redistributive solutions should include a conception of recognition and vice-versa, that encompasses the complex formation of social identities rather then one that endorses reification. Fraser's concepts are relevant to this article to facilitate an understanding of the struggles for redistribution and recognition of asylum seekers and refugee women. In the nexus of the injustices of redistribution, and lack of social, cultural and political recognition, it might be possible to position the struggles of asylum seekers and refugee women. Accordingly there is a need to look in different places for new ways in which asylum seekers and refugee women have engendered resistance to destitution (redistribution) and cultural stereotypes (recognition).

This paper explores the case of a group of African women asylum seekers and refugees in Nottingham[1], UK and their alternative forms of resistance and belonging through an informal coalition with existing charity organizations and women's groups that led to the foundation of their own non-governmental organization, African Women's Empowerment Forum, AWEF. The story here is one of activism situated in everyday life, particularly through organizational and social networking. The women's cause comes to life out of critical self-reflection and awareness of the women asylum seekers and refugees' experiences of exclusion, discrimination, and oppression. This paper aims to discuss the politics of belonging and processes of agency in the space of everyday life among a group of asylum seekers and refugee women of African origin in the UK[2]. This paper argues that the women's activities is a form of grassroots activism, which empowers women as individuals and as a community[3] contesting exclusionary systems of representation and participation, by expanding their resistance beyond the boundaries of their homes into the public sphere. It will be divided into four sections. The first briefly contextualizes the feminization of migration; the second will attempt to explore the politics of belonging and agency in the everyday life of the migrant African women; the third part will set out the methodological context; the fourth part will tell the story of the creation of AWEF – the organization as a 'home place of belonging' and women's practices of identification and networking.

**Feminization of migration**

Over the past forty years, migration, forced or otherwise, as a result of the geopolitical relations between the global north and south, has changed the face of western Europe. The main reaction from governments to the increase in forced migration is to restrict entrance into developed countries and containment methods in the developing world. In the last decade the UK government has created significant new asylum and immigration legislation, which makes granting asylum very difficult.

According to Yuval-Davis, one of the characteristics of the 'age of migration' is the feminization of migration. She states that 'the 2004 world survey on the role of women in development states that forty-nine per cent of all migrants are women' (Yuval-Davis 2009, p. 2). Research on migrant women (Sales 2007; Palmary et al 2010) has showing that, although women are victimized in different situations in the new country, they also work in the junction between oppression and agency to create a better life. In all cases, women both want and need to work (and many want to study), but are not allowed due to their migration status. This results in problems ranging from economic destitution to poor health, to cultural exclusion and to disenfranchisement. This condition is further exacerbated when one looks at their reasons for migrating, which is mostly politically or economically motivated. The continuing adverse political and economic conditions in parts of Africa have led to substantial migration overseas. In these difficult circumstances they have started a life in a new country. The experience can be alienating and traumatic as it involves a break from their familiar environment and cognitive understanding of the world. Immigration is not only crossing territorial borders but also a cultural, social and psychic boundary and enters into a new relationship in new spaces, the borderlands (Tastsoglou 2006).

The amount of institutions, associations, and organizations that have recently developed around African identity, exacerbated by various territorial and other conflicts, is puzzling. In a global world with economic interdependency and economic and social disparities, among other problems, contemporary migration flux out of Africa is attributed to the failure of nation-states to provide political, social, and economic security to the people (Manger and Munzouli 2006). Similarly the increase of non-governmental organizations caring for ethnic and displaced groups relates to western states' decreasing political will to provide social services for its citizens and non-citizens. Some commentators consider these non-profit organizations core to the exercise of agency of civil society in democratic societies (Rifkin 1995, cited in Merrill 2006, p. 157). However, critics of this view are concerned with the emphasis on the economic and social role of non-governmental organizations as there is an opportunity to remove part of the responsibility from the state and public agencies as main providers of social services (Craig and Mayo 1995). In addition, non-governmental organizations can also be a sphere where social inequalities are reproduced (Bryan 2002, cited in Merrill 2006, p. 157).

**Migrant African women: belonging and agency in everyday life**

The politics of belonging are relevant to an understanding of the trajectory of the African women's exercise of agency. Kannabiran (2006), in her investigation of the cartography of resistance of the Dalit women and their national federation in India, argues that the politics of belonging 'encapsulates within itself the politics of becoming' which occurs 'when a cultural marked constituency, suffering under its current social constitution, strives to reconfigure itself by moving the cultural constellation of identity/difference then in place' (Connolly 1996, quote in Kannabiran 2006, p. 55). In the wider scope of the politics of becoming, African women asylum seekers and refugees perform as actors rather than victims of society, and AWEF becomes the process and space where the politics of becoming/ belonging takes place. In this way, belonging refers to both formal and informal experience; not only to the cultural domain – identity and recognition – but also to economic redistribution. Moreover, and relevant to an understanding of the story of the African organization, is a conceptualization of belonging as the social place constructed by 'identifications and memberships, and the ways in which social place has resonances with stability of the self, or with feelings of being part of a larger whole with the emotional and social bonds, that are related to such places' (Anthias 2006, p. 21). The politics of becoming and belonging as discussed here refers to a 'self-conscious movement – a re-invention of the 'we' towards a goal of belonging better somewhere else' (Kannabiram 2006, p. 57).

> In this scenario one should be able to understand the migrant 'other' in ways that appreciate their modes of dealing with the reality of everyday life (De Certeau 1984), as well as the complex processes of multiple identities and belonging that so often shape the tensions and anxieties carried by those who have experienced migration and displacement. The African women's form of political struggle goes beyond the issue of identity and is based on a solidarity formation which acknowledges the translocational positionalities, 'complexly tied to situation, meaning and the interplay of

our social locations' (Anthias 2006, p. 29). In this respect the everyday becomes crucial as a site of contradictions where acts of solidarity, power, alienation and possible resistance are experienced and enacted, as well as a resource for competing reactions and coexistence of both strategies and discourses of belonging and non-belonging (Karner 2007, p. 125). In other words, how migrant women position themselves in everyday life to create an organization to negotiate their political identifications and belonging.

The everyday of migrant women is mostly negotiated in the convergence of different cultural influences and constrained by different power structures. Their experiences are lived 'outside' and 'inside' a 'displaced space'. This space is constructed by several axes of differentiation and inequality – nationality, class, gender, ethnicity (Brah 1996) – or, put otherwise, constructed and lived as a 'translocational positionality'. The complex positionality faced by people in the intersection of multiple identity locations, such as that of migrants, should be understood as 'a social process related to practices where positionality is 'the space at the intersection of structure (social position/social effects) and agency (social positioning/meaning and practice)' (Anthias 2001, p. 635). Positionality in turn becomes an intermediate term between structure and agency, which involves not just locations but also understanding of the ways in which individuals intersubjectively organize, represent or perform identification.

The forms of practices of agency performed by these women relate to Knudsen's view on how power is used in intersectionality theory; in Foucaultian sense that power might be linked to both inclusion and exclusion. That is, power is not only about suppression but could also be productive. Thus exclusion would 'involve discourses of opposition and productive power with negotiations about the meaning of gender, race, ethnicity, etc' (Knudsen 2006, p.67). In turn, agency for some of these women is about being 'conscious actors, not passive subjects in the various situations in which they find themselves' (Ralston 2006, p. 184). Self-determination in these circumstances entails a counterpoint between 'authentic' self-recognition and social acknowledgement (Taylor 1994). These notions become fundamental to an understanding of the translocational position embedded in the lives and practices of the agency of migrant women.

**Methodological context**

My theoretical approach combines elements of cultural studies with social theory by engaging with the literature on diaspora, refugees and migration, with a particular focus on women migrants, belonging, and agency in the context of everyday life. The purpose of the discussion is to challenge the invisibility of forced migrant women's grassroots struggles while widening the standard conceptualization of politics, – politics based on the public, official actors and workings of governments – to focus on 'the community-based struggles of people to gain control over their lives (Feldman and Stall 2007, p. 8).

AWEF's story represents only a small part of the results of a three years' research based on participative action combined with principles of feminist research. According to O'Neill and Harindranath, participative action research is a:

> social research methodology that includes the subjects as co-creators of the research. The ethos of PAR is based on inclusion, participation, respecting all local voices, and community driven sustainable outcomes. PAR is a process and a practice directed towards social change with the participants; it is interventionist, action-oriented and interpretive (2006, p. 46).

Moreover, O'Neill argues that:

> participatory methodologies offer potential to promote recognition, participation and inclusion in the production of knowledge and public policy. Such methodologies help to challenge dominant discourses and hopefully feed into public policy at local, regional, national and international levels (O'Neill 2010, p. 21).

To sum it up, for Fals-Borda (1995, p. 1): 'what you finally have in your hands with PAR is a purposeful life-experience and commitment combining academic knowledge with common people's wisdom and know-how'. The feminist research political ethos, which I attempt to follow in my endeavour, is research for women rather than about women (Allen and Baber 1992, p. 4) and the intention is not only to observe and describe women's lives but also to begin 'to draw attention to the political and social struggles of women' (Small 1995, p. 946).

I worked with African women asylum seekers in Nottingham while they created and developed their organization. The aim was to trace these women's struggle to establish a voice through the creation of their organizational space as well as to support their cause. The premise was that although asylum seekers and refugee women's experiences are mostly marked by subordination and disempowerment, they have the ability and will to reshape and reconstruct their identities, negotiate experiences of belonging and non-belonging and act as conscious agents toward changing their lives. Instead of offering generalizing arguments, I chose to focus on a core group of committed women engaged in multiple and interconnected organizing efforts.[4] The qualitative case study allowed me to gather an understanding of the situation of these women, and the changes that have occurred during this time in relation to identity negotiation, political and cultural belonging, and agency. A multiple methodological approach (Castells 1983) was used including interviews, focus group, participant observation and short documentary filmmaking to gain a breadth of understanding. I value participants' collaboration and recognize the importance of their distinctive input with their practical knowledge and experience about the social phenomena investigated.

My social class and race position was not a major issue with the women I engaged with although, at times, I had to explain to few of the newcomers the reasons I was there working with them. Occasionally, I would be referred to as 'the nice white lady' but I did not read too much into it as there was a general feeling of acceptance on both sides and I would like to think that there was a silent mutual agreement to respect our distinct positions while working together. My relationship with some of the women developed a few years before I even thought about doing research with them. By the time I proposed the research project, the trust was already generated. During the research process there were occasions when I was asked to help with issues related to health, security, fund raising, and so on, which were important moments to confirm my commitment to their cause and to develop further our relations of trust and respect.

The interviews and focus groups involved long conversations (i.e., ten individual interviews and four focus group interviews – average of three to five women per group). A snowball sample approach was used to reach the women; I started with the few women I knew from previous encounters. They then introduced me to other members of the group. The participants of the interviews were women coming from several parts of the African continent, particularly from areas torn by political conflicts. Their ages spread between eighteen and fifty years, with different levels of formal education, work experience, and cause of migration. A bibliographical method directed the interviews, which were participant-led in terms of the direction of the conversations and willingness to reveal their stories. The questions were organized following Feldman and Stall's methodology (2007). They thus provided an overview of the woman's family, education, work, migration history, description of their life in the new country, an examination of involvement with the group (in terms of activism or voluntary work), including aspiration and motivations for community work, understanding of the problems faced by asylum seekers and refugees and expectations for the future. In the focus groups, we explored issues related to asylum/refugee policy and its effects on their lives, notions of home and belonging, identity, prejudice and racism, destitution, 'banal' forms of resistance in their everyday life, and aspirations to change the future. As part of the participant observation process, I attended meetings and events on a regular basis, such as skill development workshops and social gatherings.

The analysis of the material was constructed reflecting a thematic nexus of migration-women-agency-belonging. The explanatory framework used grounded theory developed during data collection through observation (Charmiz 2006; Morse et al 2008). An initial set of categories of analysis for interviews were organized according to Brah's (1996) four modalities of difference: experience, social relations, subjectivity and identity. Feldman and Stall summarize these modalities as:

> experience as related to symbolic constructions in struggles over material conditions and meanings; social relations as contexts for systematic relations mediated by institutional discourses and practices; subjectivity as the site of self-in-the-world sense making; and identity as coherent, and stable (Feldman and Stall 2007, p. 104).

In my analysis, among other elements, these modalities of difference were helpful in identifying how women's perception and experiences of being 'different' might have influenced their awareness and will to change their situation of destitution and lack of recognition. By and large, the research process was very dynamic as simultaneously I collected, coded, and analysed data to inform the next phase of the investigation.

## Telling a story: African women empowering forum in the making[5]

The tension between African migration caused by political problems and the increase in non-governmental organizations due to western nation-state failures, as mentioned earlier, is reflected in AWEF. This organization is positioned at the intersection of an increasingly multicultural Europe, which is constituted by new forms of alliance and interethnic politics. It could be suggested that AWEF is an example of a 'postcolonial grassroots politics' (Merrill 2006, p. 156) that represents numerous differences – ethnicity, class, nationalities, gender, and ideologies. The process of creating the organization, which would typify a community space of advocacy, took a while. A small group of asylum seeker and refugee women discussed their situation and possible solutions to improve their material conditions in meetings among themselves and with other supporting organizations. In 2006 they produced a 'constitution' according to which they, as African women, could represent themselves. As put by one of the interviewees:

> With a group of fellow women we formed the African Women's Empowerment Forum because we experienced first hand the issues

that asylum seekers have to deal with – the prejudices, racial discrimination and oppression in society particularly in issues that affect women. I would meet with other women like me at the Victoria shopping centre because we had nowhere else to go. Many times we cried together when we talked about our situations and wonder what we could do. We started to help each other... (interviewee A).

AWEF's headquarters is situated in the city centre of Nottingham, next to the railway station, in a three-floor building provided by the local authorities. AWEF pays rent to share the premises with several non-governmental organizations. The daily work of running AWEF, from cleaning to cooking to coordinating events, to public relations, is supported by women's voluntary work. I also worked as a volunteer, and after the research ended was elected vice-chair of the AWEF Trustee Board.

The aims of the Forum are to 'advocate for women's rights and empower them through education and training'. The organization was created to 'stir them to speak out and challenge inequalities in society; to advocate for women on gender issues, equality of access and non discrimination, based on race, gender, age or immigration status'; to have an input on policies locally and nationally; and to promote a sense of belonging as well as value being responsible citizens in a foreign land' (AWEF 2006, p. 3). The organization is funded by different sources including the Nottinghamshire Foundation, the Community Champions and local authorities.

AWEF is proactive in engaging women on cultural issues and general integration into local and British society, in assisting children of African origin to maintain their identity and confidence to become responsible citizens. Their association with the voluntary sector is important to the development of their wider network of support with which they form long or temporary alliances. Partners range from the Nottinghamshire Black Partnership, the Red Cross, Rainbow Project, and City of Sanctuary of Nottingham, to local universities, among others.

AWEF is also a space for recreational, social, religious and cultural celebration of difference, as well as of commonalities within a British cultural context. Different occasions bring together Africans and people from different ethnicity-nationality-gender and give the women a sense of cultural belonging, solidarity (without denying the conflicts) and an awareness of their positionality in the new society:

We have functions together, cook Zimbabwe food, play African music[6] – just socializing. It makes me feel at home, feel like I'm part of a family. It gives me a sense of belonging and in that process we also feel that Nottingham is now our home... we share common things of Africa but we belong to different cultures and this generates conflict. It is a challenge to us (interviewee B).

Recently the organization conducted a survey among members in order to ensure that their programme is focused on their needs and that it impacts positively on the community it serves. The findings show that 95 per cent are asylum seekers without legal status; 3 per cent have refugee status; and 2 per cent are migrant workers on work permits. The majority (76 per cent) are between 31 and 60 years old. 12 per cent are between 21 and 30, and 8 per cent are younger than 20 years old. The women come from Somalia, Democratic Republic of Congo, Sudan, Zimbabwe, and Malawi. 75 per cent of the women have children, mostly teenagers. 25 per cent of children are under 5 years and 30 per cent are aged between 6 and 12 years old. About 55 per cent out of 242 members have had to leave children at home. Most live in deprived areas of the city of Nottingham. The women in the survey are educated to high-school level with 60 per cent having diplomas for specific professions such teachers; 35 per cent have degrees and 5 per cent have postgraduate qualifications. Most of the women are unemployed as they do not have permission to work but many are working as volunteers for AWEF. Only 5 per cent are in paid work. They have been in the UK on an average of 5–10 years. 85 per cent of the women suffer health problems including stress, blood pressure, and respiratory problems (AWEF 2008).

## AWEF as 'home place' of belonging

The starting point is perhaps to think of their organization (both as a process and as an institutional space) as a 'home place' in the expression of both power and resistance for African women. This concept of 'home place' as a space of resistance was developed by hooks (1990). Her proposition was that historically, African-Americans' struggles to make and sustain a home place and community offered more than providing for the daily needs; it also had a 'radical political dimension...despite the reality of domination, one's home place was the one site where one could freely confront the issues of humanization, where one could resist'(p. 42). This role of space appropriation in the expression of daily resistance is grounded in the work of Foucault's proposition that places are not only sites of dominance; they are also sites of resistance (1979). Places and spaces reflect both 'the desires of some groups of people to reproduce the social order in which they are dominant, as well as the attempts by those without such power to resist and survive in a way that is meaningful in their lives' (Wolf 1990 p. 3, cited in Feldman and Stall 2007, p. 12).

The association of these displaced women became their 'home place' where they interact with other women displaying a communal identity, whether it is religious, national, regional (African) or ethnic. Consequently, they share their cultural and political vision, concerns, and seek support for their social problems. For them, a physical place to call home (organization) is rather crucial to develop bonds with both the social and the physical environment of their new home. In this case, the importance of the home place (as a place of belonging and becoming) exceeds the necessity of functional and material support for shelter and security as attested by interviewee A:

> We became stronger as a group and they gave me strength to keep going. The organization is our home, is our shelter, our 'mother' as we cannot leave down our things to the authorities to listen [resolve] to us.

Moreover, having a personal political space to voice and share their stories was facilitated in the process of participatory research, which allowed all those involved to reflect on the different layers of the process taken place – action for changes. As O'Neill emphasizes 'engaging and connecting with feelings, intellect and politics that mediate the tensions between emotion and materiality can help us to understand better the "micrology" of migrants' live' in the wider socio political context of migration. (O'Neill 2010, p. 170) Given the connections between what Fraser (2008) refers to as redistributive and recognitive injustice and Knudsen's argument on the power of exclusion to produce agency, it is understandable that, in order to confront the oppressive reality they face, AWEF women have extended their resistance beyond the local and into the public sphere by actively engaging with policy-makers, non-governmental organizations, local and national governments to create awareness of the problems faced by asylum seekers:

> We have suffered discrimination and even verbal abuse in the streets. Apparently Nottingham has a high level record of discrimination but I must say that we managed to influence a number of agencies to support us (interviewee C).

The daily running of AWEF is expressed by many of the women in a family idiom – home place and 'mother'– cultivating and mobilizing the social bonds to develop the organization. However, women's partnership around gender and ethnic experiences of commonality is also marked by diversity. Diversity generates at times, tensions due to their conflicting ideologies, histories, and social positions inflecting on their basic similarities. These women come from diverse political, generational, cultural, religious and class backgrounds, thus differences also reflect pre-existing and continuing differences associated with pre-existing socio-geographical dynamics. Mostly, it seems they have learned to negotiate their differences, through acknowledging tensions. The women's commitment to the wider cause, as well as their strong emotional ties, supports their participation in shared activities beyond difference and occasional tensions.

*Practices of identification and networking*

For these African women the process of migration to the UK has led to a fundamental negotiation of identities, resulting from the located politics of becoming that then shapes the politics of belonging and alters the idea of community symbolized by the creation of AWEF. The awareness of multiple identities associated with different forms of belonging has reshaped many of these women's identities. The complexities of these processes are hard to pin down and can only be suggested. For many women, migration meant a loss of autonomy and freedom, even though many were running away from situations of political upheaval in which their lives were endangered. For others, migration opened up possibilities of self-improvement in spite of the difficulties faced in the new country:

> I was a successful lawyer at home but here I couldn't work and was destitute, which was very depressing. When I got my refugee status I decided to study and got a MA degree in law. Now I am working at a law firm in an apprenticeship before I can work as a full lawyer (interviewee C).

Political empowerment can be perceived in the organization's activities where there is an underlying urgency for the women to reinvent and redefine themselves in order to place a legitimate group identity before society. Thus, the incorporation of a cultural identity is implicated in the genesis of a newly institutionalized 'African women asylum seekers' political identity. In addition, networking with other organizations has helped many to develop civic and political skills (political in a wider sense), build interpersonal trust, foster feelings of belonging, and reconstruction of their identities. They have also developed a healthy relationship with the local print and broadcast media who cover most of their events in a positive tone with in-depth stories showing their resilience and hard work[7]. At the organizational level, networking reinforces AWEF as an active social actor in the migration sector as well as a build up for the interactive network of multi-layered communication systems of communities. This is what Castles (1997) calls 'women of communities' to include the host of feminist organizations, support networks, clinics, refuges and cultural associations that support women in need.

Only in the last two years have AWEF women started to use information and communication technologies (ICT). Their web page appeared in 2010, with the slogan 'educate a woman and empower a nation' (AWEF 2010) resonating perhaps a traditional utilitarian vision of women in relation to the (new) nation or perhaps just a marketing strategy where a sense of nationalism is hinted but not explicit towards any particular nation. The website's aim is to develop a local, national and transnational conversation with other 'sister' organizations to articulate a polyvocal dissent based on common concerns and successful stories to a wider audience. The ability to gain a voice in the online territory, as a discursive space, is rather valued by the women as it reinforces their empowerment as an ethnic group (Mallapragada 2006).

AWEF has come to advocate a modern identity that involves both the management of mainstream knowledge and skill systems' for its members and the creation of an economic venture based on the members' national, ethnic, gender and migration legal status. This modern identity can be observed at three levels. Firstly, in certain respect, AWEF is a formal organization with a set of rational, instrumental concerns, relating to mobilizing resources and achieving specific aims that position them in the political sphere. Secondly, it also plays an important social role in the everyday life of African women; the women promulgate ethical behaviour, and campaign against racism and discrimination, which are entrenched in daily-life activities blurring their public and private lives, and making connections with the local, the national and the global. Thirdly, the organization is a non-profit business speaking a different idiom, which is infusing everyday talk, especially at moments when women strive to craft a means of survival by presenting what is the 'asylum seeker brand' with what is their 'African life-style' in terms recognizable to others (Comaroff and Comaroff 2009). The language or public discourse of the organization is also positioned in terms of business management and what they can offer to the community, knowing over time, that they will be subjected to the attentions and measurements of the local authority community workers as well as the wider society. As interviewee A points out:

> We need to have a strong business approach to address the authorities. To talk about our "stories" is not enough anymore. We have to present what we are doing (organization) with records, plans etc. Refuge is now an industry.

For the AWEF women, asylum seeker and refugee identity is a recent social construct that matters only at a certain level, as what counts is establishing a recognized presence as a confident, future-oriented ethno-organization based on solidarity. In fact, for many of its members, AWEF has become a term of self-reference. It describes an imagined cultural community that is itself transnational, bringing together many of the African countries into Britain. The project initiated by the women is reaching towards a sense of collective political and cultural entity. In that way the organization is able to achieve its mission to help maintain an identity based on an appeal to difference, while closing the gap between them and the wider community by preserving the emotional, cultural, political and communitarian ethos of their enterprise.

Following Comaroff and Comaroff's (2009) analysis of African ethnicities, it can be suggested that in the process of its creation and consolidation, AWEF has somehow naturalized the trope of identity, which the womens' struggle for political belonging and cultural recognition so strongly highlights. Thus African women asylum seekers and refugees once dispersed have become an 'African women's empowerment forum' replete with a sense of ethno-national-engendered identity, its own agency to change lives, and its own home place (organization) to make it a reality. Combining a language of homeland and ethnicity, with migration status and the business ethos in pursuit of an African space in the UK, their claims on particularistic, and universalistic rights requires both the incorporation of identity and a cultural essence to realize, recognize, and accomplish itself. It is a 'living tautology': without the first, it would have no independent materiality; without the second, it would be indistinguishable from any other species of [non-governmental] enterprise (Comaroff and Comaroff 2009, p. 116).

## Conclusions

This article has attempted to explore the practices of belonging and agency of a group of African asylum seeker women in Nottingham through the work of the African Women's Empowerment Forum. In looking at this particular political formation, what hopefully becomes clear is that AWEF is a new and distinct space in which a group of African women have engendered agency to secure social justice and recognition, in a process that allows for 'the politics of becoming to shape the politics of belonging and transform the idea of community itself' (Kannabiran 2006, p. 68). This process of agency also allows for a convergence between everyday and political society. In the thematic nexus of women-migration-belonging-agency it is possible to suggest that these women have constructed an organization that has changed the lives of many women[8], a work recognized in 2009 and in 2011 by the national government, and in the process, has had an impact upon traditionally received notions of women asylum seekers.

The story of AWEF is not just another story. Instead it points to what might be an important phenomenon on how local grassroots movements are challenging the invisibility of asylum seekers' and refugees' lives and expanding the notion of politics to embrace a wider notion of community politics with solidarity.

The organization has developed well because of the members' ability to negotiate and renegotiate difference, and move between different spheres and interact with different social actors in order to build their own space, which they regard as a home. Migrant life is constructed in between spaces where belonging involves the emotional, the imaginary, and the rational, all of which reflect into the cultural and political life. AWEF is the embodiment of a social space that resonates these elements by providing a context of stability to the women members regarding political and community identification.

There are theoretical and practical difficulties in analysing an emergent and complex organization that results from an interethnic alliance because of the different positionality of its members[9]. In fact AWEF's experience is not without criticism or disagreement. However it has become a good example of the exercise of a grassroots activism despite its continual differences, a form of 'integration politics from below' (Pero 2008) that challenges mainstream stereotyped ideas about refugees and asylum seeker women as victims by showing a group of self empowered women. AWEF women have developed a space formed in a double movement between 'counter hegemonic' everyday resistance and recognition of neo-liberal and capitalist forces that co-exist in society. In this context, I would argue that, in the current climate of fear of global threats and scepticism with the status quo, it is rather refreshing to see an authentic attempt to empower under-privileged women through a gender network experience of affiliation and engagement.

## Notes

1. The discussion presented is not claiming that the story told here reflects the experience of such women generally in the UK.
2. 'Migrant women' refers to a group of African women asylum seekers and refugees living in Nottingham, UK. 'African women' refers to a heterogeneous group of women of African origins with distinct histories of migration as well as different political, economic, cultural and social backgrounds.
3. Community is used as:

> rhetorically, communities may represent themselves to themselves, as well as to others, as homogeneous and monolithic, as a priori, but this is an idiom only, a gesture in the

4. This article presents an overview of some of the core issues investigated in the wider project. The three women's voices presented are of the key women at AWEF's central organization who were involved in the process from the beginning and are still involved in the development of the organization. In my view they are representative of the different aspirations, age, class and ethnic backgrounds of the wider group of women members of AWEF.

direction of solidarity, boundedness and continuity. The reality is of heterogeneity, process and change; of cultural communities as diverse symbolizations which exist by virtue of individuals' ongoing interpretations and interactions (Amit and Rapport 2002, pp. 7–8).

4. This article presents an overview of some of the core issues investigated in the wider project. The three women's voices presented are of the key women at AWEF's central organization who were involved in the process from the beginning and are still involved in the development of the organization. In my view they are representative of the different aspirations, age, class and ethnic backgrounds of the wider group of women members of AWEF.
5. The following section presents the story of the creation of AWEF articulating a narrative drawn from the interviews reflecting the points of agency, belonging, recognition and redistribution.
6. The country refers to a national identity while African refers to an ethnic identity. As a political strategy the women use the combination of the ethnic and gender markers of identity to promote their organization.
7. See for example article on AWEF on refugees week, in 2010 http://www.awef.org.uk/index.php?id=press&event=This%20is%20Nottingham%20article%20published%20by%20the%20Nottingham%20Post%20on%2017th%20June%202010%20by%20Erik%20Petersen
8. Since this article was written several women have obtained refugee status and moved on to pursue a carrier and obtain academic and professional qualifications in order to integrate into British society.
9. It is not the aim of this paper to raise these theoretical problems.

## References

ALLEN, KATHERINE R. and BABER, KRISTINE M. 1992 'Ethical and epistemological tension in applying a postmodern perspective to feminist research', *Psychology of Women Quarterly*, v.16:1, pp. 1–15. Available from http://onlinelibrary.wiley.com/doi/10.1111/j.1471-6402.1992.tb00236.x/abstract [Accessed 12 April 2010]
AMIT, VERED and RAPPORT, NIGEL 2002 *The Trouble with Community: Anthropological Reflections on Movement, Identity and Collectivity*, London: Pluto Press
ANTHIAS, FLOYA 2001 'New hybridities, old concepts: the limits of culture', *Ethnic and Racial Studies*, vol. 24, no. 4, pp. 619–41
—— 2006 'Belonging in a globalising and unequal world: rethinking translocations', in Nira Yuval-Davis, Kalpana Kannabiran and Ulrike Vieten (eds) *The Situated Politics of Belonging*, London: Sage, pp. 16–31
AWEF (AFRICAN WOMEN EMPOWERMENT FORUM) 2008 *Report on Profile of its Members*, p. 2. Unpublished work.
—— 2010. Available from:[http://www.awef.org.uk/cms/ [accessed March, 2010http://www.awef.org.uk/cms/] [Accessed March 2010]
BAILEY, OLGA. G. and HARINDRANATH, RAMASWAMI 2006 'Ethnic minorities and the politics of communication in multicultural Britain and Australia', *International Journal of media and Cultural Politics*, vol. 2, no. 3, pp. 299–316
BRAH, AVTAR 1996 *Cartographies of Diaspora: Contesting Identities*, London: Routledge
BRYAN, RAYMOND 2002 'Non-governmental organizations and governmentality: consuming biodiversity and indigenous people in the Philippines', *Political Studies*, vol. 50, pp. 268–92
CASTELLS, MANUEL 1983 *The City and the Grass Roots*, Berkeley, CA: University of California Press

CASTELLS, MANUEL 1996 *The Raise of the Network Society: The Information Age: Economy, Society and Culture*, London: Blackwell. Volume 1.
CHARMAZ, KATHY 2006 *Constructing Grounded theory: A Practical Guide Through Qualitative Analysis*, London: Sage
COMAROFF, JOHN L. and COMAROFF, JEAN 2009 *Ethnicity, Inc*, Chicago, IL: The University of Chicago Press
CONNOLLY, WILLIAM, E. 1996 'Suffering, justice, and the politics of becoming', *Culture, Medicine, and Psychiatry*, 20, pp. 251–77
CRAIG, GARY and MAYO, MARJORIE (eds) 1995 *Community Empowerment*, Atlantic Highlands, NJ: Zed Books
DE CERTEAU, MICHEL 1984 *The Practice of Everyday Life*, Berkeley, CA: University of California Press
FALS-BORDA, ORLANDO 1995 'Research for social justice: some north-south convergences'. Available from http://comm-org.wisc.edu/si/falsborda.htm [Accessed 10 July 2010]
FELDMAN, ROBERTA. M. and STALL, SUSAN 2007 *The Dignity of Resistance; Women Residents' Activism in Chicago Public Housing*, Cambridge, UK: Cambridge University Press
FOUCAULT, MICHAEL 1979 *Discipline and Punish: The Birth of the Prison*, New York: Vintage
FRASER, NANCY 2008 'From redistribution to recognition? Dilemmas of justice in a 'postsocialist' age', in Kevin Oslom (ed.), *Adding Insult to Injury; Nancy Fraser Debates Her Critics*, London: Verso, pp. 9–41
HOOKS, BELL 1990 *Yearning: Race, Gender, and Cultural Politics*, Boston, MA: South End Books
KANNABIRAM, KALPANA 2006 'A Cartography of resistance: the National Federation of Dalit Women', in Nira Yuval-Davis, Kalpana Kannabiran and Ulrike Vieten (eds), *The Situated Politics of Belonging*, London: Sage, pp. 54–74
KARNER, CHRISTIAN 2007 *Ethnicity and Everyday Life*, London: Routledge
KNUDSEN, SUSANNE V. 2006 'Intersectionality – a theoretical inspiration in the analysis of minority cultures and identities in textbooks', in Eric Bruillard, Mike Horsley, Susanne V. Knudsen and Bente Aamotsbakken (eds), *Caught in the Web or lost in the Textbook*, Paris: Institute Universitaire des Maitres de Basse-Normandie de Caen, pp. 61–76
MALLAPRAGADA, MADHAVI 2006 'Home, homeland, homepage: belonging and the Indian-American web', *New Media & Society*, vol. 8, pp. 207–27
MANGER, LEIF and MUNZOULIASSAL (eds) 2006 *Diasporas Within and Without African: Dynamism, Heterogeneity and Variation*, Uppsala, Sweden: Nordiska Afrikaininstitute
MERRILL, HEATHER 2006 *An Alliance of Women: Immigration and the Politics of Race*, Minneapolis, MN: University of Minnesota Press
O'NEILL, MAGGIE 2010 *Asylum, Migration and Community*, Bristol, UK: The Policy Press
O'NEILL, MAGGIE and HARINDRANATH, RAMASWAMI 2006 'Theorising narratives of exile and belonging: the importance of biography and ethno-mimesis in "understanding" asylum', *Qualitative Sociology Review*, vol. 2, pp. 39–53
PALMARY INGRID, BURMAN, ERICA, CHANTLER, KHATIDJA, and KIGUWA, PEACE (eds) 2010 *Gender and Migration; Feminist Intervention*, London: Zed Books
PERO, DAVIDE 2008 'Integration From Below. Migrants' Practices of Citizenship and the Debate on Diversity in Britain', Working Paper no.2, University of Nottingham. Available from: http://www.nottingham.ac.uk/icmic/documents/pero-icmic-wp-08-02.pdf [Accessed 8 January 2010]
RALSTON, HELEN 2006 'Citizenship, identity, agency and resistance among Canadian and Australian women of South Asia', in Evangelia Tastsoglou and Dobrowolsky (eds) *Women, Migration and Citizenship; Making Local, National and Transnational Connections*, Aldershot, UK: Ashgate Press, pp. 183–200

RIFKIN, JAQUELINE 1995 *The End of the World: The Decline of the Global Labor Force and the Dawn of the Post-market Era*, New York: G.P Putnam's Sons
SALES, ROSEMARY 2007 *Understanding Immigration and Refugee Policy: Contradictions and Continuities*, Bristol, UK: The Policy Press
SMALL, A. STEPHEN 1995 'Action-oriented research: models and methods', *Journal of Marriage and the Family*, 57, 4, pp. 941–55. Available from: http://academic.son.wisc.edu/courses/n701/week/small_models.pdf [Accessed 10 January 2011]
SONG, SARAH 2007 *Justice, Gender, and the Politics of Multiculturalism*, Cambridge: Cambridge University Press
TASTSOGLOU, EVANGELIA 2006 'Gender, migration and citizenship: immigrant women and the politics of belonging in the Canadian maritimes', in Evangelia Tastsoglou and Dobrowolsky (eds) *Women, Migration and Citizenship; Making Local, National and Transnational Connections*, Aldershot, UK: Ashgate Press, pp. 200–30
TAYLOR, CHARLES 1994 'The politics of recognition', in Amy Gutmann (ed.), *Multiculturalism: Examining the Politics of Recognition*, Princeton, NJ: Princeton University Press, pp. 12–34
YUVAL-DAVIS, NIRA 2009 'Gendered globalisation and social change', *In Focus*, June 22. Available from: http://barha.asiaportal.info/node/974 [Accessed 16 March 2010]
WOLF, MICHELLE. 1990 '*Whose Culture? Whose Space? Whose History? Learning from Lesbians bars*'. Keynote address, *11$^{th}$ Conference of the International Association for the Study of People and their Surroundings*, 24–29 July, Ankara: (IAPS)

# Identities in-between: the impact of satellite broadcasting on Greek Orthodox minority (Rum Polites) women's perception of their identities in Turkey

Asli Tunç and Ariana Ferentinou

**Abstract**
This study aims to shed a light on women belonging to the Greek Orthodox Christian (Rum Polites) community in Istanbul, Turkey and their perception of their identity with the help of satellite broadcasting (ERT World). This research is the first attempt to analyse Rum women's viewing attitudes and their correlations with a number of variables such as education, age, family structure, religion, occupation, and their perceptions of themselves as part of a distinctive religious and cultural entity. Since the female members of the community are heavy television viewers, television is a powerful tool to construct a social reality and a sense of self. By conducting in-depth interviews and interpretative phenomenological analysis (IPA), this study aims to reveal how this unique community makes sense of their identities and social worlds through television.

*We need to know where we live in order to imagine living elsewhere.*
*We need to imagine living elsewhere before we can live there.*

Avery Gordon

*Ghostly Matters: Haunting and the Sociological Imagination, 1997, p. 5.*

## Introduction

This study aims to shed light on women's sense of belonging to the Greek Orthodox Christian (Rum Polites) community in Istanbul and their discourses of identity, as shaped in the context of satellite broadcasting consumption. The definition of the Rum Polites (Constantinapolitan Greeks) does not fully fit into existing frameworks of analysis and conceptual categories widely used, such as minority, diaspora or refugee. This unique population has a long history that can be traced back for centuries to the Byzantine Empire, although present members of the community are mainly migrants from various Greek-speaking areas of the late Ottoman Empire. They are the non-Muslim minority in the Turkish Republic adhering to Orthodoxy maintained by the Ecumenical Patriarchate. According to an official from the Rum Orthodox Patriarchate, as of 24 March 2007, the number of the community is 4,000 in a total population of 72 million, of which 1,500 are estimated to be women. In addition, there are 280 ethnic Rums in Gökçeada, twenty ethnic Rums in Bozcaada and around 1,800 Antiochian immigrants in Istanbul. The number of Turkish-speaking Antakya Rum Orthodox Christians (Antiochians) remaining in Antakya is around 10,000. Thus, there are around 16,100 Rum Orthodox Christians in Turkey. However, only 4,300 of this Greek-speaking population fall under the protection of the Treaty of Lausanne because the Turkish state does not recognize the rest as Rum Orthodox. (Akgönül 2007). After the Lausanne Treaty of 1923, there were over 130,000 ethnic Greeks in Istanbul, Gökçeada (Imvros) and Bozcaada (Tenedos) (Dündar 2000). A thriving community of 200,000 members in the beginning of the last century but now merely 4,000, the Rum Polites have not thus far been analysed at the intersection of gender division, television viewing patterns and their perceptions of themselves as a part of a distinctive religious and cultural entity.

This research aim is twofold. On the one hand, it aims to examine the role of Greek public broadcasting, ERT World satellite television in the construction of identities among Greek Orthodox minority women in Turkey. On the other, it examines whether ERT World satellite broadcasting influences Greek Orthodox women's perception of Turkish society. The two questions are intertwined and they are positioned within a sociocultural context where television viewing represents a significant element of cultural practice and identity construction within this group.

To present the uniqueness of Rum Polites, this article begins by unfolding the historical roots of the community. Following the historical background, satellite broadcasting's role in identity construction and ERT World's influence on the Rum women's perception of Turkish society and themselves are discussed. At the end of the study, the findings of in-depth interviews are analysed to understand the correlation between the community's viewing habits of ERT World and their cultural identities torn between Greece and Istanbul.

## Tracing back the story of Rum Polites

Living mostly in their cultural microcosms does not prevent Rum Polites from carrying out their daily duties in the diverse economic life of Istanbul. In spite of their commitments outside the household or as housewives, Rum women remain heavy television viewers. That is one of the major reasons why the Rum women have been selected as the sample for this study. According to the recent study of the Radio and Television Supreme Council (RTÜK) on Turkish women's viewing habits,[1] Turkish women spend nearly 4.5 hours in front of the television set daily; 58.6 per cent of those women prefer domestically produced television series, 18.4 per cent watch news and 5.8 per cent watch daytime shows, talk shows and entertainment programmes. The least popular programmes are educational programmes, health programmes and documentaries. On the other hand, the media use of Rum women is somewhat unique. Satellite broadcasting as a relatively new phenomenon in Turkey entered most of the Greek minority households in the last two decades. This study examines the hypothesis that this development, especially the satellite broadcasting services of ERT World (Greek public broadcasting) might influence the perceptions of this minority towards Turkish society and enhance their own particular identity as Greeks. If we look at the historical roots of the community, we can see how they have always been, along with the Muslim community of northern Greece, formidable paradigms of historical heritage and how current government policies shape the fates of minorities, meaning they frequently bearing the brunt in confrontations not of their own making. The Greek Orthodox minority has practically vanished from Turkey (Alexandris 1992). The fate of the Greek Orthodox community of Istanbul is almost a mirror image of the history of Turkey beginning in the mid-nineteenth century and reaching the present day. It reflects Turkey's numerous attempts for westernization and liberalization as well as its lapses into nationalist fervour. The number of the members of the Greek community of Istanbul shot up to as high as 236,000 by some estimates just after the Ottoman sultans declared their reform decrees of 1839 and 1876 (known as Tanzimat). In the wake of these decrees, which granted equal rights to all Ottoman subjects, there was a considerable inflow of Greeks from mainland Greece, which had gained independence from the Ottoman Empire only a few decades earlier (Mazower 2000). Significant numbers of Greeks came and settled in Istanbul from the Aegean islands, Thessalonica, the area of Epirus, Macedonia and

Crete, seeking business opportunities. The beginning of the twentieth century saw this community flourish, gaining considerable control over money, banking and trade in the empire. Ottoman Greeks also succeeded in rising to high government posts, for example Karatheodoris Pasha who led the Ottoman delegation at the Berlin Conference of 1878.[2] The fortunes of the Rums of Istanbul began to take a bad turn after World War I. In 1922 after Mustafa Kemal Atatürk's armies defeated the Greek armies that had landed in Anatolia in 1919, western powers concluded the Treaty of Lausanne recognizing Turkey as an independent state. In a separate agreement annexed to the treaty, 1.5 million Greeks of Anatolia were to be exchanged with some 500,000 Muslims living in Greece and in the Aegean islands. The Rums of Istanbul, Tenedos and Imvros were exempted from this agreement after much argument. The continuing presence of the Greek Orthodox Patriarchate in Istanbul was also contested by the Turks. Following the founding years of the Turkish Republic, the Greek minority of Istanbul became the target of nationalist policies suffering under severe limitations imposed on community activities such as education, and so on. Every single confrontation between Turkey and Greece, beginning with the Cyprus problem in the 1960s, had adverse effects on the life of Istanbul's Rums. The Wealth Tax levied mainly on non-Muslim citizens in 1941, the government-provoked riots in 1955 and the expulsion of Greeks in 1967 all left traumatic effects on the psyche of the community (Alexandris 1992). In what are known as 'the incidents of 6 and 7 September', violent mobs attacked property and non-Muslim individuals in Istanbul in 1955. The main target was the Rum Orthodox community, as a result of the escalation of the crisis between Greece and Turkey over Cyprus. However, Armenians and Jews were also attacked (Güven 2006). Many Rums were extremely traumatized by the events of 1955. Years of fear and uncertainty resulting from the repressive state policies exerted on the Rums of Istanbul have resulted in an introvert psychology within the community, together with conservatism and religiosity that force Rums today to keep every practice that may have been considered discriminatory in the group and to leave no room for any criticism (Ak 2008; Prodromos 2007, p. 59).

Most Rum Polites receive their basic education in Greek in the minority schools of Istanbul. They are taught by teachers who either belong to the community or who have been sent by the Greek Ministry of Education as part of the country's system of supporting diasporic Greek schools. However, those schools are under the control of and are monitored by the Turkish Ministry of Education. Hence the principal or vice-principal of those schools is appointed by the official authorities of the Turkish Republic. Their social life and identity is closely linked to the Orthodox Church. The Rum Polites perform their religious duties freely in their churches, which have been restored during the last fifteen years after permission given by the Turkish authorities, and they often organize small groups (non-profit associations – *Vakifs*) attached to their local church where they meet, and carry out philanthropic activities. The community tends to live in a closed circuit where family values are extremely important. They tend to be apolitical as they do not have any affiliation with political parties in mainland Greece and they do not develop affiliation to Turkish political parties either. Most of them tend to see Turkish politics, such as the financial situation of Turkey, according to how much they have an effect on their own community and own lives. Their 'political' points of reference are the Greek General Consulate in Istanbul, the Greek Embassy in Ankara and primarily and historically the Ecumenical Greek Orthodox Patriarchate in Fener, Istanbul. Due to the historical, cultural, political and religious significance of Istanbul (Constantinople) for the Greek community, the Greek General Consulate of Istanbul has been granted the exceptional status of an embassy and the General Consular has the diplomatic status of an ambassador. The identity of the Rum Polites revolves around their attachment to Constantinople (also known in their vernacular as *Polis*, which means city) and their belonging to the urban areas plays a central role. The Rum women, as the rest of the community, are urban subjects and live in the traditional neighborhoods of Istanbul (Beyoglu, Kurtulus, Ferikoy, Kadikoy). Almost 30 per cent of the community is over the age of fifty-five. Those over sixty-five without the means to looking after themselves are offered care at the old people's home of Balikli Greek Hospital (BalIklI Hastanesi Huzurevi) (Akgönül 2007). More than 50 per cent of the whole community is married, 2.5 per cent are divorced and 34 per cent are single.[3] In spite of the fact that there has been a marked improvement in the political and economic relations between Greece and Turkey during the last decade, the negative perceptions of Rums (and Rum women) towards the Turkish majority have not changed much. However, the coming to power of an Islamist-rooted government in the quest to join the EU has eased the tension by implementing a series of laws in favour of minorities. In their daily lives, Rum women still retain a sense of hostility towards the Turkish people and they often say they would not dream of entering into a marriage with a Turk, although mixed marriages are not unheard of. However, the Patriarchate refuses to allow the 'christening' of a child born within a mixed marriage and refuses to approve a mixed marriage, considering it an 'adultery'.

Rum women see the Greek women as very different to themselves. As they do not share any common lifestyle or background, it is no surprise that they cannot see any commonalities. One of the most sharply formulated dimensions of the Rum Polites' identity is that it differs from being 'simply Greek' or Greeks from Greece (Elladites, i.e.

Greeks from mainland Greece) (Örs 2006). In that sense, Rum women's sceptical and sometimes hostile attitude both towards Turks and Greeks has been a great challenge for Turkish and Greek researchers trying to access them. (This will be further discussed in the methodology section below.)

While the Rum women emphasize their distance from Greeks, they feel closer to Turkish women. Strong friendships between Turkish and Rum women, especially when living in the same neighbourhood, are common. Women of Greek origin who join the Istanbul Rum community through marriage often express a sense of isolation. There is a long tradition of marriage within the Rum community. This is true even among the large community of Rums who have now settled mainly in Athens after being expelled from Turkey or left on their own for fear of reprisals between 1955 and 1974–7.

### A brief history of Greek satellite broadcasting[1]

Satellite channels first started being transmitted in Greece through the frequencies of ERT World at the end of the 1980s. The first Greek satellite (Hellas Sat) was launched in May 2003. The infiltration of satellite television in Greek households is low (under 10 per cent according to market estimates, although there are no official figures) compared to other European countries. According to AGB Hellas, satellite channels represent only 1 per cent of viewership.[4] Multichoice Hellas is the mother company of NOVA, the only subscription-paying digital TV platform. Free-access satellite channels as well as channels by subscription broadcast via the platform of NOVA reach an audience of merely 1,000 viewers. Those viewers in Greece who watch channels of free reception via a satellite aerial (dish) number approximately 150,000. To access the satellite services of NOVA (almost forty channels – besides the Greek ones transmitted both via satellite and land line), one acquires the complete equipment (dish, decoder with access to a few free channels, access card) and a monthly fee of approximately €35. NOVA is licensed to broadcast in Greece only, but many Rums manage to get it through various means. These include the illegal use of access cards, which they import from Greece or 'cracking' the access cards, and recently via the internet. Rum women indicate that Greek satellite television plays a very important part in their life in Turkey. However, they have certain reservations with regards to the programme content. The ideological underlying message in ERT World programming is reaching the 'Greeks abroad'. The target audience is mainly the Greek diaspora, which lives across the world. Rum women do not consider themselves as 'migrants' or diasporic subjects. They are indigenous to Turkey. While their cultural roots and language are Greek, they have always resided on Turkish soil and are Turkish citizens. Their homeland is Turkey. Hence, they do not have the same common social background as the rest of the Greeks who live abroad. The term 'abroad' does not apply to them, so they cannot relate to some of the programmes broadcast on ERT World such as travel programmes showing the Greek countryside, village life, Greek folkloric customs, and so on. Anything that appeals to the Greek migrants with a common memory of mainland Greece is of no particular interest to the Rums.[5]

An additional point that applies to the unique situation of the Rums is that they form an overwhelmingly urban community, as they live in one of the oldest and most populous urban centres of the world, Istanbul. Thus they do not have particular knowledge or interest about the 'village life' that ERT World focuses on in order to satisfy its target audience of Greeks abroad, most of whom have rural origins. At the same time, Rum women complain that too much television time is devoted to sports coverage on ERT World. However, ERT World is by far the channel most watched by the Rum Polites.

## Debates on satellite television viewing, global public sphere and cultural identities

In this study, the concept of 'in-between-ness' is used to explore the Rum community where their sense of belonging is a never-ending search for identity. In-between-ness refers to the constant feeling of dislocation, discussed by Bhabha (1994), Gilroy (1994) and Hall (1990) within the context of post-colonialism. As people feel disjointed from the national boundaries, their identities are shaped as a form of resistance identity opposed to their political identities as citizens (Barber 1995; Castells 2004, 2007; Lull 2007). The emergence and sustaining of contemporary global public spheres are largely dependent on new media communication systems and their mediatory role for sustaining in-between identities (Volkmer 1999; Bennett 2004; El-Nawawy and Iskander 2002; Paterson and Sreberny 2004; Dahlgren 2005; Tremayne 2007). Volkmer (2003, p. 9) also discusses 'how the media infrastructure of the global public sphere has been tremendously differentiated in recent years', framing identities along the lines of new cultural and political parameters (Castells 2001). As Fraser (2007, p. 7) rightly indicates, 'a growing body of media studies literature is documenting the existence of discursive arenas that overflow the bounds of both nations and states.' Those debates are also surrounded by the questions of cultural identities and the potential impact of satellite broadcasting (Harvey 1995; Morley and Robins 1995; Morley 2000; Robins 2006). In the post-1990s, extensive research has been conducted revolving around the concept of 'transnational communities' on cross-border television (Kang and

Morgan 1990; Straubhaar, Consuelo and Cahoon 1995; Goonasekera and Lee 1998; Lee 2000). Most of these studies have focused on Indian audiences, their identities, culture, values and their access to satellite television (Gupta 1998; Fernandes 2000; Mcmillin 2001; Butcher 2002). All of these studies pointed out that viewing television was not merely an act of consumption but was 'rather a complex process of decoding cultural meanings' (Wang, Servaes and Goonasekera 2000, p. 4). Widely used theoretical frameworks were cultural imperialism and cultural hegemony. 'Cultural imperialism is the policy of extending a nation's authority over other nations through cultural means' (Malhotra and Rogers 2000, p. 409), and hegemony denotes a 'dominant cultural order which is consistently preferred, despite its articulation with structures of domination and oppression'(Grossberg 1996, p. 161). These studies specifically point out the adaptation of western values and conditions of advanced capitalism by the 'non-western' communities. For more than two decades, satellite broadcasting has been seen as a way of 'electronic colonialism' (McPhail 1987, p. 17) with negative consequences.

On the other hand, it should be kept in mind that the role of satellite broadcasting in global communication flows is steadily growing in importance and contributes to ethnic cohesion and cultural maintenance as well as to helping members of communities integrate into a larger society (Riggens 1992). In fact, a number of developing countries' governments express concerns that satellite broadcasting might erode their sovereignty by transmitting foreign programming to their populations in an unregulated manner (Karim 2007). In addition to extensive research conducted on Indian culture, there is also research on Italian and German communities in Canada (Lofaro 1994), Arabic-speakers in Europe (Gillespie 1995; Chouikha 2007), religious groups like the Mormons, and the Jewish Lubavitch and Ahmadiyya sects in various countries such as the USA, Germany and Pakistan. Satellite channels carry out similar types of programming schedules and advertising. However, apart from those similarities in programming, the major differences lie in the languages and cultural content. Milikowski (2000, p. 460) points out that migrant viewing of television should be analysed from a uses and gratifications point of view as she observes 'non-ideological and non-political gratifications usually go a long way to explain a certain popular interest.' However, can such a simplistic approach be valid for the complex experiences of the Orthodox Greek minority living in Istanbul?

**Methodology**

This research is based on in-depth interviews conducted among thirty-two female Greek Orthodox viewers in households located in Istanbul.

Respondents were asked about the role and significance of Greek state television programming on satellite, about how their viewing habits had affected personal and family attitudes, perceptions of their identities and awareness of political developments in Greece and Turkey, and whether satellite broadcasting had been a point of identification for women, as well as how much satellite broadcasting had influenced their viewpoint on social and cultural life. The central concern of this study is the understanding of Rum women's experiences at a holistic level. The major challenge of the study was to earn the trust of the members of the Rum community. While they were assured that their identities would be kept confidential, they remained wary towards the researchers. A large research literature examines the ways in which researchers can plan a qualitative research project, conduct in-depth interviews and fieldwork, and analyse qualitative data (Mishler 1986; Burawoy 1991; Corbin and Strauss 1990; Booth, Colomb and Williams 1995; Lofland and Lofland 1995; Wolcott 1995), when the interviewee or the topic is emotionally sensitive (Corsino 1987; Campbell 2002). However, in this research, the bridge of trust had to be built between the interviewers and interviewees because of their different cultural and historical background. The Rum community in general is reluctant to interact both with the Greek and Turkish population and, for that matter, to participate in any research conducted by a Turkish and a Greek scholar. The researchers needed to consider how their own identity may have an impact on the respondents and how they might seek to probe beyond ethnic, religious and historical positions based on mistrust of the other side. Gaining trust of the community was not an easy one. Both of the researchers regularly attended masses. The Turkish researcher took Greek lessons to have a sense of the intricacies of the language, while the Greek researcher spent a considerable amount of time with the Rum women in social circles. However, the researchers benefited from community leaders' connections and recommendations to reach the community.

The series of thirty-two semi-structured interviews discussed in this study were undertaken over a period of six months with the Rum women residing in Beyoğlu, the Princes Islands, Feriköy, Bosphorus and Kurtuluş. The women were from various age groups and the interviews lasted from thirty-five to forty-five minutes. All the interviews were conducted in Greek and translated into English. All were audio-recorded and transcribed verbatim. In the pre-interview process of the Rum community, the researchers acknowledged the possibility that there might have been a degree of scepticism on the part of the interviewees, wondering 'why us?' (Bogdan and Biklen 2003), and the possibility of resisting any scrutiny 'by anyone not belonging to their own group' (Whitty and Edwards 1994). According to Adler and

Adler (2001), once respondents perceive themselves as marginalized, sensitively placed or vulnerably positioned, they are reluctant to share any information. In this framework, the Rum women, as a part of the whole Rum community, show reluctance to share their experiences, feelings and opinions with anyone not belonging to their community. Ironically, the researchers (one Greek and one Turkish) could not escape from being a part of the perception of 'us vs. them'. Although each researcher had to experience her own difficulties in contacting the community, the different identities of the researchers also enriched the scope and vision of the research. In other words, their personal feeling of being 'in-between' left a mark on the research itself.

For this study, interpretative phenomenological analysis (IPA) has been used. IPA is concerned with trying to understand lived experience and with how participants themselves make sense of their identities and social world. IPA is phenomenological in that it wishes to explore an individual's personal perception or account of a state as opposed to attempting to produce an objective record of the state itself (Smith, Flowers and Larkin 2009). In other words, IPA is concerned with trying to understand what it is like from the point of view of the respondents. The Rum female community is a fairly homogenous sample that can be studied with the use of IPA.

**Rum women's perception of their identity through satellite viewing**

*Locating the self within a nation*

The study's starting point was that identity is 'a reality in motion', 'a bundle of territorial and mental adherences', which are conjugated 'according to diverse alchemies, the local, the regional, the national, the international' (Mattelart 1996, pp. 12–7).

The Rum identity is profoundly constructed within a social context where the influence of historical heritage, community structures, the strength of the religious centre of the Patriarchate and family structures play a significant role in their combination. Community identity researchers (Cohen 1985; Wilkinson 1986; Moodie 2000; Dominy 2001; Sampson and Goodrich 2005) have tended to focus on how places are repositories of both personal and shared (symbolic) meanings that serve to distinguish communities from other groups of people. One of the major identity markers of the Rum Polites is their religious affiliations and their dedication to the Patriarchate. The other major pillar of their identity is the Greek language. Rum Polites protect and cherish their language as a tool for resistance against the dominance of the Turkish language in the city.

For the women in this study, the selection of a certain genre of programmes, such as documentaries, daytime shows or news programmes, was an important rite of signification in locating their identities within Turkish society. To be truly 'Rum Polites', they were aware that they needed to know the Greek language. For example, eleven of the respondents indicated that ERT World programmes facilitated geographic mobility in that they could 'visit' remote parts of Greece. Understanding the language provided them with a sense of belonging to the culture in Greece yet imparted to them a sense of rootedness within Turkish society. Satellite broadcasting provided the Rum women with a window into seeing Greece beyond the national boundaries of Turkey. The Rum women's relationship with ERT World satellite broadcasting does not represent an irreversible break from the Turkish mainstream TV channels, since the Rum female audiences are also heavy viewers of domestic popular serials or current affairs programmes. An Istanbul-born sixty-eight-year-old retired school teacher who lives in Kurtuluşs (Kurtulus) said: 'I have been watching ERT World for twenty years and the main reason is keeping my ties with the Greek language, culture and history and to feel that I belong both to Greece and to Constantinople.' On the question of whether they identify themselves as Rums of Constantinople, all respondents reacted by strongly emphasizing that they cannot describe themselves as anything else but that.

*A community of heavy television consumers*

Almost all respondents in this research have spoken about their heavy television viewing (at least three hours a day). The ways in which this choice was discussed made it clear that television viewing plays a significant role in their lives and in the construction of their identities. The heavy viewing was not correlated with their educational background or socioeconomic status. From the college graduate secretary of the Patriarchate to the elementary school-educated housewives or the high-school dropout gym teacher, they all indicated that they watched literally everything on Turkish and satellite television except sports programmes. Yet, they preferred to watch news and discussion programmes on ERT World.

A wealthy sixty-three-year-old with a university degree who is an icon painter and who divides her life into two by spending half of the year in Greece and the other half in Istanbul (Şişli), is a heavy viewer. As she said, she keeps the televison on all the time while working. She was almost offended when asked whether her feelings and ideas towards Greece or Turkey have been affected by watching Greek satellite television: 'I have made up my mind already. I don't need television to decide how I feel towards those two countries.' However, she thinks that watching Greek satellite television has influenced the Rum women in Istanbul on many levels. According to her, the reason for watching ERT World is to maintain her links with Greece. She feels that she belongs to Greece. She also watches ERT World to keep up with the latest developments in Greece and to be entertained. She also indicated that watching ERT World is 'the natural thing to do for every Rum who lives in the Poli (Istanbul).'

A fifty-four-year-old high school graduate who is currently working in the tourism sector and lives in the centre of the city (Cihangir neighbourhood), watches both Greek and Turkish television, but she is not interested in the political developments in Greece. Her selection of genres of Greek television resembles those she chooses on Turkish television. She watches serials, game shows, travel shows, music programmes and documentaries. She travels to Greece five times a year.

Another participant is a seventy-five-year-old housewife with an elementary school education, living in the house in which she was born and where her parents and grandparents were born. She is currently the only Rum resident of the Balat area on the Golden Horn. She is a heavy television viewer with ten hours of viewing a day. She lives alone and looks after a local church. She feels incredibly proud of her Greek and Orthodox identity and says:

> On my name day, the Patriarch himself paid a visit to my house. I have never been happier in my whole life. That gives me strength to live here until the end of my days where my parents and grandparents lived. I am totally alone. I watch television all the time. I watch Greek television mostly just because I don't want to forget my Greek.

She stays in Turkey and does not travel to Greece. The higher the level of education, the more Rum women prefer to watch both Greek and Turkish television. Respondents also stated that they follow the political developments in both countries through television programmes.

A fifty-eight-year-old university graduate high school teacher living in Şişli, indicated that since she started watching ERT World twelve years ago, she has become more knowledgeable of what was happening in Greece and at the same time the level of her Greek has improved. However, she also watches most of the Turkish channels on a regular basis and she frequently visits Greece. Drawing from a book she wrote about her family history, she describes the feeling of alienation of the community:

> [M]y biggest grief however is that while we, the Rums of the Polis, live in this place where we found ourselves for generations and generations, which undoubtedly is our land and the land where the

bones of our ancestors are buried and it is the land of our people and our families, some consider us foreigners and outsiders and are looking at us with evil eyes. We are the ones who sent our men to the Turkish Army to fight, we are the ones who never complained and never made any demands. We have always been exemplary, law-abiding, dignified citizens of this country, paid our taxes, never broke the law.

## *A perpetual love for the city of Istanbul*

The city of Istanbul occupies a unique place in the heart of all Rum community members. According to them, it has cultural, historical and emotional value. They refer to it by its Byzantine name, Constantinople, or as 'the Polis' for short. It is 'The' city for them. They describe the lifestyle, tradition, habits and social behaviours of citizens and even the architectural structure of Istanbul with a profound feeling of nostalgia. One of the interviewees said:

In the old times the city was beautiful. The Greek we were speaking was the best in the world, even better than the Greek spoken in Greece. Even the Turks were speaking Greek then. But those were different Turks. We used to be friends with each other. Today everything changed. The city is now full of Kurds from Anatolia.

When asked whether ERT World helped them in knowing their city better, most of them pointed out that serialized novels such as *Loxandra* written by Maria Iordanidou, an Istanbulite Rum who lived in the early twentieth century describing life in the Polis in the late nineteenth century, helped them feel closer to the city. Apart from serials, documentaries and travel programmes about the city also enhance the sense of belonging. Besides *Loxandra*, another popular serialized novel in a similar setting, *Hadji Emmanuel* by T. Kastanakis, was widely watched among the Rum community.

The recent Greek–Turkish rapprochement began with the destructive successive earthquakes in both countries in 1999. This generated a big interest in knowing each other's lifestyles through popular culture. A number of documentaries were produced as a result of this interest, such as *The Suspended Step of Turkey* in 2005. This was a production by the Reporting Without Frontiers team and was shown on ERT and ERT World, depicting the contemporary Rum community. Additionally, the programme *Diaspora*, produced by ERT3 based in Thessalonika, frequently covered stories associated with the Rum Polites community.

*Orthodoxy holding the community together*

The Rum women described their identities revolving around their religious routines and practices. All of them indicated how the Patriarchate played a significant role in their lives and existence within the Turkish society. They all pointed out that they performed their religious duties regularly and freely in Turkey. They rarely miss attending mass at the Orthodox church and follow the religious calendar. The church also provides them with a platform for social interaction. At the same time, they regularly watch mass on ERT World, especially those who are unable to attend physically. For instance, at the old people's home at Balikli, ERT World on Sunday mornings is always on. In that way, television becomes an alternative choice for major religious events such as Easter and Christmas mass.

**Discusssion of the findings**

In this study we have observed that the choices and interests of the Rum women tend to underline the affirmation of the 'in-between-ness' of their identity. They show special interest to subjects that have an immediate proximity (i.e. events between Greece and Turkey) or particular religious affairs associated with their own practice. They tune into ERT as the channel revives familiar forms of entertainment or representations of daily family life in Greece. Although they all said that they watch Greek news on ERT, they also indicated that they would like to see fewer political discussions that deal almost exclusively with domestic political issues in Greece. Instead they asked for more television serials, music programmes, concerts, theatre performances and comedies. They were particularly interested in historical and biographical programmes in order to 'increase their knowledge of Greek history and to know the personalities involved', as some of them said.

The findings revealed variations between different generations of Greek Orthodox women, also associated with differences in class and education. We have also observed that televised images of the city of Istanbul are received, appreciated and interpreted in ways that reinforce their sense of both rootedness and in-between-ness. Along the same lines, these women expressed significant interest in watching documentaries produced by ERT in the post-1990s that depicted their life as a minority in Turkey. The value attached to this kind of viewing in informing participants' identities is captured in the anger caused by a documentary drawing a gloomy picture of a dying community of Rums.

## Conclusion

As a conclusion, this research confirms the fluidity of the sense of belonging of a unique community and gives voice to the female members of the Rum community to define their identities through the experience of television watching. It also reaffirms the significance of satellite broadcasting for identity construction and maintaining of linguistic identities among diasporic communities. For the Rum community, their identity is torn between their linguistic and cultural affiliation to Greece and their total devotion to their beloved city that symbolizes the continuity between a historical past and a lived present. As Istanbul sustains a role as the ecumenical centre for Orthodox faith, their devotion to the city is grounded as much on urban, cultural, and religious elements of their identities. This research has also shown how demographic indicators, such as social and economic status, and educational level do not solely define their perception of their identity, especially as ERT World has opened up new ways for reflecting on their identity and its limits.

## Notes

1. These are the findings of a research on the television viewing patterns in Turkey conducted by RTÜK on 10 March 2009; 2,570 participants in twenty-one cities took part in the research. See http://www.rtuk.gov.tr
2. See http://www.megarevma.net/tarihce.htm
3. From the proceedings of Istanbulite Rums Congress, 'Istanbul'da Buluşma: Bugün ve Yarın' held at Hilton Hotel, 29 June–3 July 2006.
4. The authors are indebted to the administration of ERT World for providing us with detailed information about Hellenic Satellite Broadcasting Services.
5. See http://www.ejc.net/media_landscape/article/greece

## References

ADLER, PATRICIA A. and ADLER, PETER 2001 'The reluctant respondent', in Jaber Gubrium and James A. Holstein (eds), *Handbook of Interview Research: Context and Method*, Thousand Oaks, CA: Sage, pp. 515–36
AK, CEREN ZEYNEP 2008 'Minorities within minorities: between the "self" and the "other"', *Turkish Policy Quarterly*, vol. 7, no. 3, pp. 105–12
AKGÖNÜL, SAMIM 2007 *Türkiye Rumları Ulus-Devlet Çağından Küreselleşme Çağına Bir Azınlığın Yokoluş Süreci*, Istanbul: İletişim Yayınları
ALEXANDRIS, ALEXIS 1992 *The Greek Minority of Istanbul and Greek–Turkish Relations 1918–1974*, Athens: Centre for Asia Minor Studies
BARBER, BENJAMIN R. 1995 *Jihad vs. McWorld*, New York: Times Books
BENNETT, W. LANCE 2004 'Global media and politics: transnational communication regimes and civic cultures', *Annual Review of Political Science*, vol. 7, no. 1, pp. 125–48
BHABBA, HOMI K. 1994 *The Location of Culture*, London: Routledge
BOGDAN, ROBERT and BIKLEN, SARI 2003 *Qualitative Research in Education: An Introduction to Theory and Methods*, Needam, MA: Allyn and Bacon

BOOTH, WAYNE C., COLOMB, GREGORY G. and WILLIAMS, JOSEPH M. 1995 *The Craft of Research*, Chicago, IL: University of Chicago Press

BURAWOY, MICHAEL 1991 *Ethnography Unbound: Power and Resistance in the Modern Metropolis*, Berkeley: CA: University of California Press

BUTCHER, MELISSA 2002 *When STAR Came to Town: Cultural Change and Transnational Television in India*, New Delhi: Sage

CAMPBELL, REBECCA 2002 *Emotionally Involved: The Impact of Researching Rape*, New York: Routledge

CASTELLS, MANUEL 2001 *The Internet Galaxy*, Oxford: Oxford University Press

—— 2004 *The Power of Identity*, Malden, MA: Blackwell

—— 2007 'Communication, power and counter-power in the network society', *International Journal of Communication*, vol. 1, pp. 238–66

CHOUIKHA, LARBI 2007 'Satellite television in the Maghreb: plural reception and interference of identities', *History of Anthropology*, vol. 18, no. 3, pp. 367–77

COHEN, ANTHONY P. 1985 *The Symbolic Construction of Community*, Tavistock Publications, Chichester

CORBIN, JULIET and STRAUSS, ANSELM 1990 'Grounded theory research: procedures, canons, and evaluative criteria', *Qualitative Sociology*, vol. 13, no. 1, pp. 3–21

CORSINO, LEONOR 1987 'Fieldworker blues: emotional stress and research underinvolvement in fieldwork settings', *The Social Science Journal*, vol. 24, no. 3, pp. 275–85

DAHLGREN, PETER 2005 'The internet, public spheres, and political communication: dispersion and deliberation', *Political Communication*, vol. 22, no. 2, pp. 147–62

DOMINY, MICHELE 2001 *Calling the Station Home: Place and Identity in New Zealand's High Country*, Lanham, MD: Rowman and Littlefield

DÜNDAR, FUAT 2000 *Türkiye Nüfus Sayimlarinda Azinliklar* [Minorities in the National Census of Turkey], Istanbul: Çiviyazilari

EL-NAWAWY, MOHAMMED and ISKENDAR, ADEL 2002 *Al-Jazeera: How the Free Arab News Network Scooped the World and Changed the Middle East*, Cambridge, MA: Westview

FERNANDES, LEELA 2000 'Nationalizing "the global": media images, cultural politics and the middle class in India', *Media, Culture & Society*, vol. 22, no. 5, pp. 611–28

FRASER, NANCY 2007 'Transnationalizing the public sphere. On the legitimacy and efficacy of public opinion in a post-Westphalian world', *Theory, Culture & Society*, vol. 24, no. 4, pp. 7–30

GILLESPIE, MARIE 1995 *Television, Ethnicity and Cultural Change*, London: Routledge

GILROY, PAUL 1994 'Black cultural politics: an interview with Paul Gilroy by Timmy Lott', *Found Object*, vol. 4, pp. 12–25

GOONASEKERA, ANURA and LEE, PAUL S. N. 1998 *TV Without Borders – Asia Speaks Out*, Singapore: Asian Media Information and Communication Centre

GORDON, F. AVERY 1997 *Ghostly Matters: Haunting and the Sociological Imagination*, Minnesota: University of Minnesota Press

GROSSBERG, LAWRENCE 1996 'History, politics, and postmodernism: Stuart Hall and critical studies', in Morley David and Chen Kuan-Hsing (eds), *Stuart Hall: Critical Dialogues in Cultural Studies*, London: Routledge, pp. 151–73

GUPTA, NILANJANA 1998 *Switching Channels: Ideologies of Television in India*, New Delhi: Oxford University Press

GÜVEN, DILEK 2006 *Cumhuriyet Dönemi Azinlik Politikalari ve Stratejileri Baglaminda 6-7 Eylül Olaylari*, Istanbul: Iletisim Yayinlari

HALL, STUART 1990 'A place called home: identity and the culture politics of difference', in Rutherford Jonathan (ed.), *Identity: Community, Culture, Difference*, London: Lawrence & Wishart, pp. 222–238

HARVEY, ROB 1995 'Survival by satellite: television boosts resolve of smaller religious groups living in sometimes hostile cultures', *The Ottawa Citizen*, C5, 25 February

JONATHAN, SMITH A., FLOWERS, PAUL and LARKIN, MICHAEL 2009 *Interpretative Phenomenological Analysis: Theory, Method and Research*, Newbury Park, CA: Sage

KANG, JONG GUEN and MORGAN, MICHAEL 1990 'Culture clash: impact of US television in Korea', in Martin John and Ray Eldon Hiebert (eds), *Current Issues in International Communication*, New York: Longman, pp. 293–301

KARIM, KARIM H. 2007 'Nation and diaspora: rethinking multiculturalism in a transnational context', *International Journal of Media & Cultural Politics*, vol. 2, no. 3, pp. 267–82

LOFARO, TONY 1994 'New, mini-satellite dishes appeal to ethnic viewers', *The Ottawa Citizen*, 5 February

LOFLAND, JOHN and LOFLAND, LYN H. 1995 *Analyzing Social Settings: A Guide to Qualitative Observation and Analysis*, 3rd edn, Belmont, CA: Wadsworth Publishing Company

LULL, JAMES 2007 *Culture-on-Demand: Communication in a Crisis World*, Malden: MA: Blackwell

MCMILLIN, DIVYA 2001 'Localizing the global: television and hybrid programming in India', *International Journal of Cultural Studies*, vol. 4, no. 1, pp. 45–68

MCPHAIL, THOMAS L. 1987 *Electronic Colonialism: The Future of International Broadcasting and Communication*, Newbury Park, CA: Sage

MALHOTRA, SHEENA and ROGERS, EVERETT M. 2000 'Satellite television and the new Indian woman', *Gazette*, vol. 62, no. 5, pp. 407–29

MATTELART, ARMAND 1996 *The Invention of Communication* (p. 3), Minneapolis, MN: University of Minnesota Press, p. 3

MAZOWER, MARK 2000 *The Balkans: From the End of Byzantium to the Present Day*, London: Phoenix Press

MILIKOWSKI, MARISCA 2000 'Exploring a model of de-ethnicisation the case of Turkish television in the Netherlands', *European Journal of Communication*, vol. 15, no. 4, pp. 443–68

MISHLER, ELIOTT G. 1986 *Research Interviewing: Context and Narrative*, Cambridge, MA: Harvard University Press

MOODIE, JANE 2000 'Preparing the waste place for future prosperity? New Zealand's pioneering myth and gendered memories of place', *Oral History*, vol. 28, no. 2, pp. 54–64

MORLEY, DAVID 2000 *Home Territories. Media, Mobility and Identity*, London: Routledge

MORLEY, DAVID and ROBINS, KEVIN 1995 *Spaces of Identity. Global Media, Electronic Landscapes and Cultural Boundries*, London: Routledge

PATERSON, CHRIS A. and SREBERNY, ANNABELLE 2004 *International News in the 21st Century*, Eastleigh: University of Luton Press

PAUL SN, LEE 2000 'Television and global culture: assessing role of television in globalisation', in Anura Goonasekera, Jan Servaes and Wang Georgette (eds), *The Communications Landscape, Demystifying Media Globalisation*, London: Routledge, pp. 188–98

PRODROMOS, YANNAS 2007 'The human rights condition of the Rum Orthodox', in Zehrak. Arat (ed.), *Human Rights in Turkey*, Philadelphia, PA: University of Pennsylvania Presspp. 57–72

ROBINS, KEVIN 2006 *The Challenge of Transcultural Diversities. Cultural Policy and Cultural Diversity*, Strasbourg: Council of Europe Publishing

SAMPSON, KAYLENE and GOODRICH, COLIN 2005 'We're coasters, why should we move?': community identity, place attachment and forestry closure in rural New Zealand', *Sites*, vol. 2, no. 1, pp. 124–49

STEPHEN HAROLD, RIGGENS 1992 'The media imperative: ethnic minority survival in the age of mass communication', in Riggens Stephen Harold (ed.), *Ethnic Minority Media: An International Perspective*, Newbury Park, CA: Sage, pp. 1–20

STRAUBHAAR, JOSEPH, CONSUELO, CAMPBELL and CAHOON, KRISTINA 1995 'From national to regional cultures: the five cultures and television markets', *Social Scientist*, vol. 28, pp. 322–3

TREMAYNE, MARK 2007 *Blogging, Citizenship, and the Future of Media*, London: Routledge

VOLKMER, INGRID 1999 *News in the Global Sphere: A Study of CNN and Its Impact on Global Communication*, Eastleigh: University of Luton Press

—— 2003 "The global network society and the global public sphere", *Journal of Development*, vol. 46, no. 4, pp. 9–16

WANG, GEORGETTA, SERVAES, JAN and GOONASEKERA, ANURA 2000 *The Communications Landscape, Demystifying Media Globalisation*, London: Routledge

WHITTY, GEOFF and EDWARDS, TONY 1994 'Researching Thatcherite education policy', in Walford, Geoffrey (ed.), *Researching the Powerful in Education*, London: UCL Press

WILKINSON, KENNETH P. 1986 'In search of the community in the changing countryside', *Rural Sociology*, vol. 51, no. 1, pp. 1–17

WOLCOTT, HARRY F. 1995 *The Art of Fieldwork*, Walnut Creek, CA: AltaMira Press

# Index

References to tables are in **Bold**

access to legal assistance 18
activism: AWEF 116; ethnic media 70
African life-style 127
African women 116–129; agency 118–9, 128–9; belonging 118–9, 128–9; every day 119
African Women Empowerment Forum (AWEF) 116, 122–8; activism 116; advocacy 122; aim 123; assessment 129; consumption 135; home place of 124–6; modern identity 127–8; organization, as 127; proactive engagement 123; running of 125–6; space 125; survey 124; uniqueness 134–5, 139
age: differences 106
agency: African women 118–9, 128–9; culture as site of 41
Ali, Suki 5
ambivalence 90
anatomy of silence 17–20
antagonism 106
assimilation 48
audiences 79–81; Arab 82–3; heroines 82–3;media savvy 86; sense of community 88; soap operas 79–83; stranger 93
authentic self-recognition 119
autonomy, loss of 126
axis of differences 63

Bailey, Olga Gudes 7, 115–129; methodology 119–20; modalities of difference 122; thematic nexus 122;
belonging 111; African women 118–9, 128–9; African Women Empowerment Forum 124–6; phantasmic 109; sense of 104
binary oppositions 61

bonding attitudes: Flanders 55–6; Netherlands 51–2
boundary work 32–3
bridging attitudes 57; Flanders 55–6; Netherlands 51–2

cartography of resistance 118
census profiles 37
China 27, 34, 33–7; community media 35
Chistensen, Miyase 7, 97–112; frame 98–100; methodology 98–100; study 98–100
circulated truth 5
Citizenship Referendum 2004 29–30
citizen body 14
city: origin, of 104; residence, of 104
civil engagement, decline of 46
classist discourse 86–7
commonality of identity 106
communication 11–14; rights 12–13
confidence 69
confidential communication 17
conservative values 90–1
consumption 90–1; Greek Orthodox Church 135; soap operas 79,81
continuity; external 2–3; internal 2
cosmopolitanism 97, 100–112; analyses 100–3; expressions of 103; typology 110
constituting news 36
contrapuntal theory 28, 40–1
Corporate Responsibility Report 2007 33
counter hegemony 129
critical cultural studies 6
cross-border television 139
cultural: corruption 109; hegemony 140; injustices 116; integration 29

# INDEX

dedication to Patriarchate 142
definitions; citizenship 4; social capital 45
demographics: Flanders 53; identity 147; indicators 147; Netherlands 50
D'Haenens, Leen 8, 44–58; methodology 49–50; research questions 46; results 50–6
diaspora 77, 79, 84–93, 99, 102, 104, 111; origin, and 81
different life trajectories 36
direct integration thesis 47
distance 78, 82, 85–7
domination 63, 65–72
double absence 61

economic interdependency 117
electronic colonialism 140
ERT World 143–5, 139
essentializing attitudes 109
ethnic media: activism 70; alternative 70; design 70–1; discrimination 71; individuality 71–2; practices 70–2
European character 115–6

female: escapism 89; labour force 15–16
feminism 63–4
feminization of migration 15; African women 117–8; Ireland 31
Ferentinou, Ariana 8, 133–147; challenges 140; methodology 140–2
financing 19
fixity 103; transcultural fluidity, vs 97
Flanders 45, 47–50, 53–56; bridging attitudes 55–6; bonding attitudes 55–6; demographics 53; gender differences 51–2; media use 55; religious attitudes 55–6; social capital 55
free movement 11
fourth generation rights 12
fractured oppositions 61
framework 9
freedom, loss of 126
French-speaking countries 65–6

German-speaking countries 65
gender: differences 51–2, 55; hierarchies 84
genre proximity 87
Georgiou, Myria 1–9, 77–93; methodology 83; participants 78
ghetto-thesis 47
globalization 10

grass-root struggles 120, 122
Greek Orthodox Christian (Rum Polites) 134–147; back story 135–8 dedication 142; education 136–7; family values 137; identity; 136–7, 142–5; language 142–3; love for Istanbul 145; orthodoxy 146; perceptions 142–6; politics 137; preferred genres 146; riots 136; Turkey, and 137–9; women 137–8
group consciousness 79

heavy television consumers 143–5
Holocaust camps 11–12
home place: resistance, as 124
human rights 12

identity: demographic indicators, and 147; formation, 97, 100–9, 111–12; Greek Orthodox Church 136–7, 142–5; inter/intra-group 102, 108; middle-class 85–6; social construct of 128
ideological interest 6
illocutionary inclusion 14
immigration policies: criminalization 17; securitization 17
imperialism hegemony 140
in-between-ness 139, 146
information, free flow 3
interculturalism 32
interdisciplinary crossroads 3–5
inter/intra-group; identities 102, 108; positions 102, 108
international: news 39; political economy 14–17
Interpretative Phenomenological Analysis 142
intersectionality 5, 62–72
Ireland 27, 29–33, 37–40; culture 31–2; domopolitics 29–31; governance 31–2; integration narrative 31–2; labour force 29–30; policies of integration 29–33
Istanbul 135–7, 139; perceptual love for 145

journalistic practices 66–9; distinctions 66–7; diversity of specialization 68–9; soft news 68

language 57; classes 48–9; Greek Orthodox Church 142–3
legal voice 21
legitimacy of existence 12

# INDEX

living tautology 128
locating self within a nation 142–3

material: virtual, and 104–7, 111–12
mainstream media 66
mass media 46–47; access to 67–8
matrix of domination 11
meanings of place 97, 100, 104, 111
measures of bonding **52**
measures of bridging **53**
media: ecology 3; fragmentation 4; literacy 85–6; use 50–1, 54
mediated: communication 3–5, 98, 100–4, 111–12; identities 63–5
melodrama 80–1
Migrant Rights Centre 2010 Report 30
migration rates 15
mobile agency 109–10; gender, and 108, 111–12
mobility 108, 111–2
modern identity; AWEF 127–8
modernization 82
multiculturalism 31–2;failure 8,21; resistance to 48–9
multiple identities 4; struggle 72
Muslim studies 99

national ideals 31
neo-assimilationist agendas 29
Netherlands 45, 47–56; bonding attitudes 51–2; bridging attitudes 51–2; demographics 50; gender differences 51–2; media use 50–1; religious attitudes 52; social capital 51–2
new: borders 17–20; trends 62
Nigeria 27, 33, 37–40
non-EU citizens 27–8
nostalgic discourse 87

Ogan, Christine 8, 44–58; methodology 49–50; research questions 46; results 50–6
online; communication 46; media 107
operation of camps 19
orthodoxy: Greek Orthodox Church 146
otherness 2, 14, 31, 105–6, 111, 115
Ottoman Empire 135–6

particularism-universalism continuum 88–9
personhood 11–14
political empowerment 126–7
positionality 119

positions of responsibility 69
post-colonial relations 63
practices of identification 126–8
practices of networking 126–8
production-accumulation cycle 16
produsage 103
proximity: critical 78, 89–92; cultural 77–8, 80–2; 87–9
public sphericules 4
Putnam, Robert 44–6

Radio Telifis Eireann 33
recession 30
redistributive solutions 116
reflexivity 89, 99, 108, 110
religious attitudes: Flanders 55–6; Netherlands 52
representation of women 72–3
reproduction of inequality 72
retraditionalization ideologies 82
rights: communication 12–13; fourth generation 12; second generation 12; social 13; speech 13–14
Rigoni, Isabelle 7, 61–73

sacrifice 21
Sarikakis, Katharine 6, 10–21
satellite broadcasting, Greek 134, 138–146; history 138–9; NOVA 138; target audience 138–9
satellite television viewing; cultural identities, and 139–40; debates 139–40; global public sphere, and 139–40; roles of 146
second-generation rights 12
secularism 90–1
self, the 2
self-determination 119
sexual: harassment 69; violence 11, 17
shared history 80
silencing 12, 18
soap opera 77, 80–3; audience 79–83; banality of 86, 93; consumption 79, 81; critique of role 91; movement struggles 64; politics, and 90–2; popularity 84; success 81
social;:acknowledgement 119; alienation 105–6; capital 44–57; categories 63–5; centrality 104; construct of identity 128; contact 58; marginalization 6; rights 13, 18; trust 47; visibility 108
space of self-representation 65
spatially-defined limits 111
speech: refusal to 19; rights 13–14

## INDEX

stereotypes 61, 58, 69, 116
Sweden 97, 102–6; spatial segregation 105
symbolic: existence 21; role 104

technology 3–4, 46–7; AWEF 127
television: Arabic 77–93; viewing 46–7
territory of existence 20
Title, Gavan 6, 27–41; methodology 34; participants 34–5, 38–9
transcultural fluidity; fixity vs 97
transnational 101–4, 106, 112; debate, locating 6–9; gender dynamics 108; locality vs trans-locality 97–100; migrant settings 100–4
triangle of dehumanization 20–1
Tunc, Asli 8, 133–147; challenges 140; methodology 140–2

Turkey 45–56, 97, 102–4, 106; Greek Orthodox Christian, and 137–9; liberalizat5ion 135; westernisation 135
two-way process 28

UK legislation 117
under-studied 65
'us vs them' 142

value system 87
vertical segregation 69
virtual; material, and 104–7, 111–12
voice 12
volatile changes in EU countries 18

world shrinking 20

Printed in the USA
CPSIA information can be obtained
at www.ICGtesting.com
LVHW011138150324
774517LV00040B/1656